ADDITIONAL PRAISE FOR *DIGITAL OPERATING MODEL*

"As companies increasingly adopt digital-first business strategies, *Digital Operating Model* becomes a must read for business leaders who want to harness the power to disrupt their markets and avoid being disrupted. An insightful, practical guide to achieving digital maturity and reaping the promise of competitive advantage and exponential growth."

—IAN WORDEN,
MBA, MHI, Chief Product Officer, Sandata

"Not only does Rajesh Sinha provide expert advice, but he also provides firsthand accounts where these mantras are already generating exponential growth for modern businesses. The lessons learned transcend industry and are valuable to any entrepreneur."

—AARON PRICE,
CEO, TechUnited: NJ; Founder, Propelify

"The *Digital Operating Model* offers an excellent in-depth account of how some of today's industry leaders are harnessing the power of digital to accelerate business growth. Having worked with countless clients worldwide, Rajesh Sinha shares invaluable lessons he's learned along with his knowledge and experience in a way that makes transformation plausible, possible, and successful no matter the company or industry."

—YURI AGUIAR,
author of *Digital (R)evolution: Strategies to Accelerate Business Transformation,* and Chief Enterprise Data Officer, WPP

Digital Operating Model

Digital Operating Model

The Future of Business

Rajesh Sinha

WILEY

Published by John Wiley & Sons, Inc., Hoboken, New Jersey.
Published simultaneously in Canada.

Library of Congress Cataloging-in-Publication Data

Names: Sinha, Rajesh (Digital Strategist), author.
Title: Digital operating model : the future of business / Rajesh Sinha.
Description: Hoboken, New Jersey : Wiley, [2022] | Includes index.
Identifiers: LCCN 2022011362 (print) | LCCN 2022011363 (ebook) | ISBN
    9781119826835 (cloth) | ISBN 9781119826859 (adobe pdf) | ISBN
    9781119826842 (epub)
Subjects: LCSH: Internet marketing. | Technological innovations.
Classification: LCC HF5415.1265 .S555 2022 (print) | LCC HF5415.1265
    (ebook) | DDC 658.8/72—dc23/eng/20220412
LC record available at https://lccn.loc.gov/2022011362
LC ebook record available at https://lccn.loc.gov/2022011363

Cover Design: Wiley
Cover Images: © Christopher Yin, Pablo Viera Zunino

SKY10034702_061622

*To my wife, Vandhana, and son, Pranay, who are my pillars
and whose support keep me grounded.*

To my late father, who planted the seeds of entrepreneurship within me.

To my mom, my family and friends, and my Fulcrum family.

Contents

Preface

A company's success depends on its digital strategy today and into the future. Disrupt or be disrupted is the mantra as businesses of all sizes rush to digitalize and deliver better experiences for employees and customers.

Digital is not a myopic approach to utilizing the latest technology to automate a business process. It's a holistic shift that embraces the potential of the business platform through the digital operating model—a proven successful pathway to digital maturity.

The digital operating model—DOM—revolves around three crucial elements: culture, business platform, and innovation. Culture lays the foundation for a business platform, and together both help a business remain relevant through innovation. Knowing the nuances of this interconnectivity in the digital world helps a business better position for the future.

When all three foundational elements are aligned and working together, a business gains the momentum necessary for the journey to digital maturity. That's DOM in motion and the result is bottom-line growth.

As lifestyles, workplaces, and demographics change, and businesses move toward on-demand goods and services, development and deployment of the multilevel DOM has become essential. Companies that don't make the shift to the digital mindset and reusable, reconfigurable business platforms can't move fast enough, lose their relevance, and quickly fall behind the competition.

Many leading companies of a decade ago are different today, and they will be different tomorrow. That's changed the dynamics of what's necessary to deliver on the rapidly changing demands of consumers. The digital operating model levels the playing field. Any company now can have the platform power to take on big players, disrupt, and win.

In 2010, the market leaders in the Fortune 100 by market capitalization included legacy giants like General Electric, Ford Motor Company, J.P. Morgan, and Bank of America Corporation. By 2021, technology giants as well as innovators and changemakers like Alphabet, Apple, and Amazon had displaced stalwarts like General Electric, Exxon Mobil, Walmart, and AT&T from the top spot. By 2030, the picture could change again as companies that focus on building a digital culture, organizing their businesses as platforms, and embracing innovation are ready to win again.[1]

This is the guidebook to help any company remain relevant today and ready for the future of tomorrow. In these pages leaders and experts from all size companies—with revenues from a few million to billions of dollars— and across varying industries share their stories of what works on the journey to digital maturity, what doesn't, and why. They offer sage advice and guidance for others as well.

Readers will learn step-by-step the details of the DOM and its five levels to continuous digital maturity. The top level of performance—continuous digital maturity—happens when a company moves at a high velocity and can pivot as markets and economies dictate, and easily and smoothly incorporate the latest technologies into their business ecosystem.

The five levels to continuous digital maturity are:

- Digital infancy
- Early experimenters
- Digitally credible
- Digitally mature
- Market leaders

Digital Operating Model: The Future of Business gives readers clarity on why culture, platform, and innovation are so important, and what it takes to move any company to the next DOM level of performance. You'll learn how to assess where your company is on its own digital journey, and how to turn that assessment into the right road map for your company to maintain the momentum necessary for growth—DOM.

The digital operating model is the result of my three decades of experience in digital entrepreneurship and software. Since the software business has a proven multilevel engineering model, I figured why not a multilevel company maturity model for the digital journey. And so, the DOM approach with its five levels to maturity was born.

The book is divided into four parts:

- Part I introduces readers to the concept that the impossible is possible with the power of the digital operating model.
- Part II shares the secrets of how any company can build its own digital operating model, use it as a road map, and achieve digital maturity.

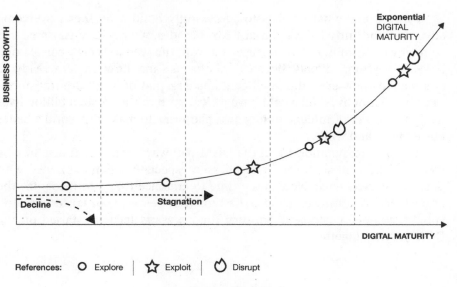

Pathway to Growth

- Part III shares with readers how crisis can create opportunities that enable savvy companies to make the right moves now to get ahead of the competition and propel themselves into the future.
- Part IV looks at future business trends and technologies of today and tomorrow, and how companies can remain relevant and avoid being disrupted.

Throughout these pages there also will be case studies that explore how companies of different sizes and industries have overcome challenges and reached various levels of digital maturity. The end of each chapter includes Pathways to Growth, vital takeaways that offer a roundup of key points on any company's journey to embracing the digital operating model.

So many people have contributed their knowledge to this book. Combined with expertise from nearly two dozen CEOs and leaders, who share their behind-the-scenes challenges and opportunities in these pages, you and your company can be the disruptor in your industry. Outsiders don't have to come in with the latest and greatest. Your company can have the innovative foresight and digital savvy to transform and grow.

Over the years, my teams and I have worked with and helped thousands of companies create thriving cultures and achieve digital maturity. We understand the journey, know the nuances, challenges, and pitfalls, and how to triumph. Working with so many companies, we've also learned that all share these three common denominators on the digital journey—culture, platform, and innovation.

I also know what it takes to successfully build a business, overcome adversity, and thrive. Over the last two decades, we have transformed our company's digital maturity. It's evolved from the web to social, portal, analytics, everything digital, business platforms, and now we are ready to embrace the new era—the intelligent business platform. We are transforming 100 million lives today and have a clear path to transform a billion lives using the power of intelligent business platforms to make the world a better place to live and work.

The business platform and the DOM pathway opens the future to new ideas and new possibilities for businesses, especially when combined with purposeful excellence. Now is the time to embrace it and to recognize the importance of putting experience first for your people, your customers, and your customers' customers. So, turn the page and let's get started on the DOM journey together.

Acknowledgments

This book is an amalgamation of stories, experiences, and wisdom from 23 successful business leaders and CEOs who join me to bring this book to you. They are my cohorts and friends. Each invested many hours and days and months to complete their own stories so that others might learn how to reimagine their businesses.

So many people contributed so much to this book—from information and stories to cover designs—that it's not possible to list everyone. My sincerest gratitude to all of you. I also would like to especially thank:

Paul Stoddart, President, New Payment Platforms, Mastercard, UK

Marc Adee, CEO, Crum & Forster, USA

David Granson, Managing Director, Goldman Sachs, USA

Gary McGeddy, President, Accident and Health division, Crum & Forster, USA

John Binder, President, Commercial Lines division, Crum & Foster, USA

Tom Bredahl, President, Surplus and Specialty division, Crum & Foster, USA

Paul Whitcomb, CEO, Whitsons Culinary Group, USA

Beth Bunster, CFO, Whitsons Culinary Group, USA

Nick Saccaro, President, Quest Food Management Services, USA

Bobby Floyd, CEO, HHS, USA

Peter John, Vice-Chancellor and Chief Executive, University of West London, UK

Adrian Ellison, Associate Pro-Vice Chancellor and CIO, University of West London, UK

Said Hathout, CEO, Al Hilal Life, Bahrain

Vishakha R M, CEO, IndiaFirst Life Insurance, India

Joe Santagata, CEO, American Carpet South, USA

Paul Hopkins, Programme Director, NHS England, UK

Steve Butcher, retired, Head of Procurement and Shared Services, Higher Education Funding Council for England (HEFCE), UK

Brennon Marcano, CEO, The National GEM Consortium, USA

Yuri Aguiar, Chief Enterprise Data Officer, The WPP Group, USA/UK

Rudy Sayegh, CEO and Founder, Global Gate Capital, Switzerland

Andrew Zaleski, President, Breakwater Treatment & Wellness, USA

Cesar Castro, Founder and Managing Partner, Escalate Group, USA

My wife, Vandhana, and son, Pranay, played the most important roles in supporting me so that I have been able to build my business and share the magic of DOM with you.

My sincere thanks to both my parents for giving me this life and having confidence in me throughout.

My friend and colleague, Dhana Kumarasamy, and his family have stood behind me like a rock during the highs and lows.

My three siblings and Lalit Khandelwal and their families have played an important role as well.

Business colleagues who have supported behind the scenes: Mark Blemings, Ian Joubert, Arleen Paladino, Nicole Bennett, and Rohan Sharan.

The business networking group of YPO and my YPO Forums have played a pivotal role in shaping me as a person.

I have become friends with many customers and associates of my company over time, and they have become my extended family, mentors, and advisors.

Most importantly, I would like to thank the team who helped me organize the facts and stories:

Sheck Cho, Susan Cerra, and the team from Wiley; without their support I could not be on this journey of authoring a book.

Susan J. Marks for her support in this journey from start to finish.

To my biggest family (Fulcrum), who have contributed so much to this book: Christopher Yin, Abilash Krishnaswamy, CP Jois, Munishk Gupta, S. Mukundhan, Bhimesh Karadi, Christine Rota, Mecca-Amirah Jackson, Matt Norrito, Pablo Viera Zunino, Christopher Vaccaro, Sachin Panicker, Adam Morris, Anthony Latona, Vinay Rawat, Anuradda Jayanntha Banerjii, Michael Kinder, and all the global leaders and employees of Fulcrum.

The book wouldn't be complete without also extending my gratitude to all the people from my Fulcrum family and those who have directly and indirectly helped me on this project. Without their support, I would not have achieved so much.

PART I

THE IMPOSSIBLE
IS POSSIBLE

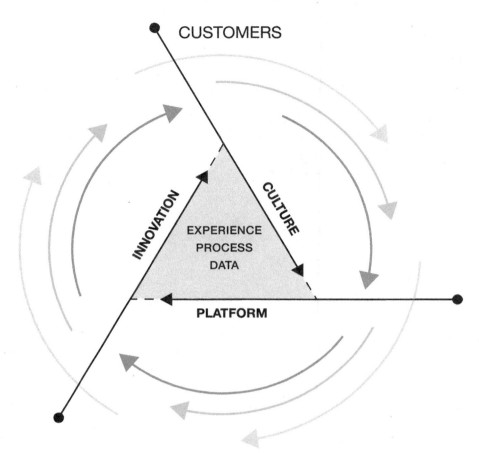

CUSTOMERS

INNOVATION

CULTURE

EXPERIENCE
PROCESS
DATA

PLATFORM

EMPLOYEES

INPUTS
Platform
Innovation
Culture

OUTPUTS
Customer
and employee
experience

Digital Operating Model

CHAPTER 1

Your Mantra for Success

The digital operating model is not for the privileged.
It's for everyone.

Digital strategy is the differentiator today. For any size company in any industry, the choice is disrupt with the power of the business platform or be disrupted.

Consumers want better, faster, and more seamless experiences. They expect goods and services on demand; they want more control of their data; and they like making their lives easier and better. Digital platforms do all that plus have the power to generate growth that companies once thought unimaginable.

DOM AS YOUR GUIDE

The digital operating model—DOM—is the step-by-step pathway for your company's journey to digital maturity (see facing page). It spells out how any company can transform more lives effectively and efficiently with digital ecosystems that are available, accessible, and often without massive cash outlays or personal technology expertise.

Three Common Denominators

For a company's successful digital maturity, three key elements, or common denominators, must be present. That foundation of the DOM is:

- Culture—the people mindset to embrace the adoption of new ideas and the speed that digital enables to deliver on constantly evolving consumer needs. A great culture fosters trust, helps your people thrive, and delivers exceptional customer experiences.
- Business platform—the right technology to run business processes—both horizontal (employee-facing) and vertical (customer-facing), creates multiple outcomes, and delivers new ideas with speed. The platform enhances data accuracy and security, generates metrics and measurable key performance indicators, and provides a built-in road map for the future.
- Innovation—the openness to come up with and welcome new technology, ideas, and processes—to fail fast, learn, and grow in the process. Innovation can be internal, as in making lives and processes easier for your employees, or external with the goal to improve customer experiences.

Culture is the first step that enables a company to embrace the right business platform and open the door to innovation. The alignment of all three elements powers the momentum to drive business acceleration, more and better customer experiences, and growth to achieve the five levels to digital maturity. That's DOM in motion and the pathway to transformation. In these pages you'll read many stories of businesses that set out on the journey. For those that succeeded, all three elements aligned.

Five Levels in the DOM

DOM identifies five levels of achievement on the journey to continuous digital maturity—the ability of a company to seamlessly and quickly react to market shifts and demands no matter the circumstances.

Those five levels are:

- **Level 1: Digital infancy.** New or legacy businesses with little automation; no conclusive **culture** outside of authoritative tendencies; nonexistent **platform** technology; preoccupied with day-to-day activities; little **innovation** or exploration.

- **Level 2: Early experimenters.** Primarily new or marginally established businesses of varying sizes; no clear company direction; no structured road map; often trapped by a slow-growth mindset and technology-hesitant **culture**; some systems manual, others automated; data largely disconnected with siloed business **platforms**; management considering **platform** and integration solutions; too preoccupied with manual process and siloed systems to drive **innovation**.

- **Level 3: Digitally credible.** Some success but DOM organizational principles not fully adopted; utilize many of the latest technologies; routinely challenge themselves to do better; actively seek additional investment and opportunities to break out of linear growth; rely on digital road map; decentralized, growth **culture** well-communicated to employees who actively seek improvements; business **platforms** yield benefits but not fully integrated vertically and horizontally; showing signs of **innovation**.

- **Level 4: Digitally mature.** Clear direction mapped; frontline and senior management in alignment; comfortable with next-generation business platforms; easily explore, exploit, and occasionally disrupt; positive growth-centric **culture** with employees who value company's work and success levels; well-integrated vertical and horizontal **platforms** and can measure their impact on customers and employees; committed to continuous growth and **innovation** and learning from past experience.

- **Level 5: Market leaders.** Highest level of digital maturity; continuously establishes new and surpasses previous benchmarks; either disrupting market leaders or are market leaders; DOM principles on full display; purpose-driven **culture** that embraces transforming people's lives; organization seamlessly integrated horizontally and vertically with end-to-end business platform; takes advantage of **platform** and market-derived data and monetizes and extrapolates it to the fullest; **innovation** hard-wired into people, processes, and vision.

DOM helps a company understand the step-by-step approach to digital maturity. It's a tool to assess digital readiness and chart a road map for transformation. Sound too good to be true? It's not; it's reality, and not a technophile's dream. DOM helps technical and even non-technical professionals implement fluid digital and growth strategies so that their companies can become disruptors. The complex becomes simple with the digital operating model.

YOUR BUSINESS AS A PLATFORM

The COVID crisis prompted almost all of us to recognize the importance of virtual connections as we struggled to run our businesses remotely. Those who did so successfully learned that the process begins with knowing the business end to end. Once someone has that organizational clarity, it's possible to reimagine the possibilities and, with the power of the business platform, chart a path to transformation.

The best way to do that is think of your company operating on a business platform as like a shopping mall, see Figure 1.1. To meet the company's needs, rather than run down the street to get one thing, across town for something else, and a couple of miles in another direction for still more, everything that is required for operations is in one place. It's like a shopping mall delivered on any channel. Everything is a click away on the digital platform.

And if something isn't there today, stay tuned. It will be tomorrow because the system or business platform, with its built-in resiliency, is designed to adapt to changing needs.

Shopping malls came about for customer convenience and experience, with everything needed in the same place. That means horizontal services like food management, parking, and restrooms conveniently located, as well as vertical services like the availability of various types of stores and products offered for purchase. Building your business as a platform provides the same convenient approach with one venue, inside of which instead of many and varied stores and options, are your company's departments, services, and applications. The platform provides and enhances everything a company needs from internal support systems—those horizonal business systems that serve your teams' needs—to external experiences provided to customers.

After all, the success of a shopping mall depends on the quality of the customer experience; the same is true with your business built as a platform. A well-built shopping mall with the right services in the right place and easily accessible (horizontal and vertical applications) provides smooth traffic flow and a pleasant customer buying experience. The well-built business platform offers smooth data flow and provides a positive user experience.

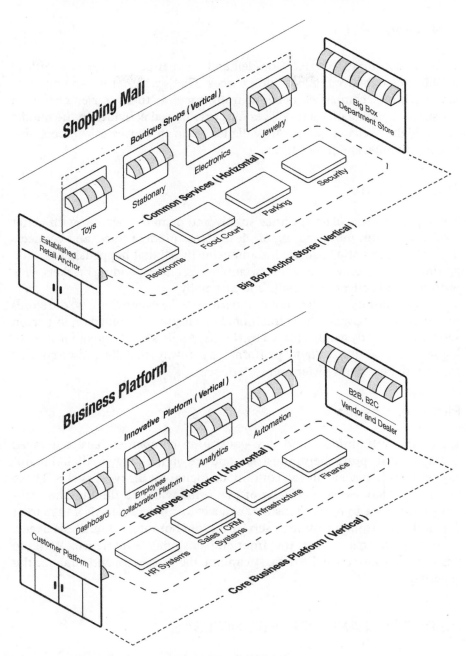

FIGURE 1.1 Build your business platform like a shopping mall.

A NEW WORLD

Today's consumer expects on-demand, hyper-personalized (artificial intelligence-enhanced) goods and services. That's whether it's an employee tapping into a company's network from home at their convenience or a consumer hopping on their devices for personalized activities in the middle of the night. Welcome to this new digital world that gives easy access anywhere, anytime, and in any format.

The Right Link

The right business platform links supply and demand together with better products, creates more sharing of ideas across product lines, and connects multiple aspects of a business instantaneously. All that happens while integrating efficiencies with customers, employees, and expanding markets. This is on-demand delivery internally and externally.

Brick-and-mortar video rental stores used to be everywhere; so did stores that sold vinyl records. Those traditional businesses that relied on in-person services are mostly gone, replaced by Netflix, Apple Music, and other streaming services that utilize digital platforms as pathways to deliver more content along with better and easier user experiences.

Platform Results

Today, many traditional and new-generation companies have embraced DOM, are disrupting their industries, and are on their way to digital maturity or already have achieved continuous digital maturity—Level 5. Those Level 5 companies have clusters of platforms with the fluidity and technology expertise to respond instantaneously to customer needs and market demands. Horizontal platforms service backend or internal business needs. Vertical platforms deliver the front-end customer experience. Working together they monetize the data, streamline the processes, and enhance the experiences.

DISRUPTION AND OPPORTUNITIES

Disrupt or be disrupted isn't necessarily only about embracing the new and different or innovating with the new and once-thought-impossible on the way to upend the status quo in an industry. It's also about recognizing that sometimes revising or nuancing an existing process can disrupt, too.

Companies don't need to wait for an outsider to deliver the disruption that makes traditional products and services obsolete. Almost any big box retailer could have created its own version of Amazon years ago if it had the vision and innovative foresight, thought through disruption, and embraced the digital operating model with the ability to scale. Any large or small hotel or lodging group could have created its own version of Airbnb long before the latter was a force.

And, with the right digital platform, taxis could have morphed into their own version of rideshare services long before other newcomers cornered the market. Instead, all were left to scramble, to react to an outsider bringing in change and disruption.

With the power of business platforms any company can become the disruptor in an industry and experience exponential growth.

THE FACE OF DISRUPTION TODAY

In these pages, CEOs and leaders of real companies will share their insights gleaned from their own extensive digital journeys. They'll share how their companies embraced DOM and have achieved a certain level of maturity, as well as what's ahead on the transformative path. They'll talk about the importance of remaining relevant, what's required to create multiple digital accelerators, and how to realign a company's culture with this new digital mindset.

You'll quickly see the difference that developing an intentional strategy to embrace the DOM can make for any business. However technology alone is not a silver bullet and rarely solves every problem a company faces, according to Ian Worden, a 20-year veteran healthcare and IT product executive involved with cutting-edge digital change.

It's just one tool in the toolbox, says the long-time innovation and strategy leader. The game-changer is understanding how to find the value in technology as an enabler and how it can be leveraged. That's especially true given the advances in artificial intelligence (AI)—as in speed and accuracy—that in some cases can't be replicated by human actions.

Growth Through Automation

HHS is a $700 million hospitality organization that needed to dramatically improve its productivity and cut back on human error. Both were limiting the Dripping Springs, Texas-based company's ability to serve customers, grow, and innovate.

For more than four decades the company aggressively expanded to provide thousands of facilities worldwide with services like end-to-end catering, health and safety, patient flow, and more. HHS serves more than 750 partner organizations, including healthcare, resort, senior living, government, aviation, and education industries.

But the company's process, data, and experience had fallen behind because of its overdependence on manual tasks like supply chain distribution, HR payroll reviews, and financial statements. These tasks stalled productivity, increased human error, and detracted from time spent on value-creating innovations essential for growth.

Platform transformation. With the implementation of a well-thought-out digital platform solution, the company transformed. Utilizing robotic process automation—software technology/robotics (bots in the jargon) to handle certain interactive tasks—the company netted an 89% cost savings; achieved a 99% reduction in errors; and allowed 28 employees to again focus on creating new and innovative ideas.

The digital operating model has enabled HHS to give back to its managers a lot of time that used to be spent on manual tasks, says company CEO Bobby Floyd. Some of the positive changes that have benefited from more automation include streamlined training, initial onboarding, and competency testing.

Better experiences. Moving to a digital platform also helped HHS enhance its customers' experience. It was a situation of *you don't know what you don't know.* Platform-enabled data gave HHS new insights into efficiencies and deficiencies.

Labor constraints always have been a big driver of actions, says Floyd. A big chunk of the company's business is in healthcare, where the rising costs of providing care mix with decreased reimbursement. Because of that, he says, it's important to become efficient and effective with the available labor resources. That's especially true from a frontline perspective.

For example, one of the company's clients is a hospital in Nashville, Tennessee, where HHS's responsibilities include linen distribution. A laundry processes and delivers linens to the hospital, then HHS staff distributes them where needed, puts them away, and removes the soiled linens. It's not "very sexy," says Floyd. But, it is extremely costly and important.

"One of the things we implemented at the hospital was a digital platform to field requests from clinicians on floors so that we would know what linens were needed in what department," he says. "Early on, before the digital platform, the surgery department would call every day to request additional laundry pickup and delivery. That meant that every day management had to reallocate labor—pull one person away from something else to service the surgery department. We [corporate and scheduling] didn't know it was happening, though, because every day the phone call was to a different person."

Once on the digital platform, linen requests along with all the other operations and staffing data suddenly became available and visible online. For the first time, Floyd says, his teams could see the actual call volume and identify the problem—regular repeated calls from the surgery department. The situation was quickly rectified with a simple schedule change.

The rules of engagement have changed. It's embrace disruption or be disrupted.

Furniture Manufacturing

In 2019 when Ari Asher became Chief Operating Officer (COO) of New York-based U.S. operations for Global Furniture Group, he inherited a legacy ERP (enterprise resource planning) system. It was homegrown and about 30 years old. GFG manufactures office furniture in Canada, and has marketing, sales, and distribution in the United States.

Asher's bosses in Canada wanted him to make it easier for customers to do business with the company—a rather broad task. "We sell furniture in a company that uses an aging IT technology, but we also shop on Amazon, and interact with our bank digitally today. So, as consumers we're used to something as all our customers are, so we need to address or meet or try to exceed these expectations when they come to deal with us," says Asher.

Initially, Asher considered suggesting replacing the aging ERP system in part to fix issues involving unnecessary manual labor demands. But, he says, "At the end of the day you look at the toolbox you have, you look at where you can improve and become more efficient. At least from my perspective you never fix broken process with technology. First, you make sure the process is as clean as possible and then apply technology to make it more efficient, more user-friendly, to make it more acceptable."

And that's what Asher, his teams, and the executive leadership have done and are still doing incrementally as the company transforms on its DOM journey from Level 3 and nearing Level 4. Changes in how invoices are audited is just one example of how GFG has matured its processes on its digital journey. Instead of 15 people manually auditing invoices, today the process is automated via digital platform and involves just two people. It's a move that saves the company hundreds of thousands of dollars annually.

"As managers I think it's irresponsible to continue operating a fat organization because you are just not delivering enough to the bottom line," Asher adds. "By strengthening the company, we are actually taking care of the employees, too."

Such is the potential and the power of DOM in motion.

HISTORY REVISITED

Today's DOM-enabled journey to connect products and commerce with consumers isn't so very different from the connectivity journeys of ancient history.

The Spice Trade

Thousands of years ago, spices were a valuable commodity that was monetized. Pepper was a trading currency like gold.[1]

Countries, traders, and merchants sought pathways to pick up and deliver their precious cargo—including spices—from distant lands like China, India, and the Middle East. Ships, barges, and people transported the spices via age-old pathways, rivers, and canals, as well as across oceans, and around the horn of Africa.[2] Traders expanded their market opportunities by leveraging the various pathways. Innovators sought new and more efficient routes for commodity procurement and delivery.

Enhanced Pathways

As the traditional system of oceans, waterways, and paths expanded over time, obtaining spices became easier, faster, and more efficient. Spices lost their extreme value as a commodity, and were replaced as a currency by gold, coin, and paper. Roads, railways, and air freight were added to the procurement and delivery system, making life even easier.

And it's still happening. In the last decade, China committed $40 billion on a Silk Road project to connect its markets with Europe through a series of roadways. While the country continues to invest in digital and technology sectors, it hopes these new pathways will reduce its dependency on waterways for the shipment of goods.[3]

The business platform has been added, too, to enhance flow and delivery. In many cases, digital has become the currency. Data is the commodity—the new gold—as we move forward in this digital age.[4]

Today, rather than physically or manually sending something from one country or one city to another, the platform reduces the time and accelerates the transaction process. People can buy and sell from anywhere; transactions can originate and scale from one location, too, and instantly—no delays.

The Evolution of Trading Currency

In the same manner that pathways have evolved historically and matured over time, the currency of trading has evolved over thousands of years, from possibly sticks and stones in the beginning of civilization to cattle around 10,000 BCE, shells and precious metals, then spices, followed by coins and paper currency. The latter was first used by China's Tang dynasty (618–906 CE).

Then came the gold standard in 1821 in England that pegged the value of currency to the value of gold. Credit cards debuted in 1946. Most recently another form of currency is growing in popularity—digital money or cryptocurrency. It's decentralized and not controlled by any organization or government. Instead, it's monitored by peer-to-peer internet protocols.[5]

A MARATHON STEP-BY-STEP

As history has shown us, these changes don't happen overnight. They take time. The move to embrace digital successfully is no different. It's not a sprint. No matter the size of the business or the industry, it's a marathon. Like a marathon the digital maturity journey requires intentional preparation, understanding, step-by-step planning, and incremental implementation to be successful.

It's also about learning how to align existing technology investments with newer initiatives to make the difference, and all without massive expenses.

Roadblocks on the Journey

Most companies that fail at the digital journey do so because of lack of planning and approach. Or they sprint out of the gate without a plan or road map and, as happens in a marathon, end up worn out and exhausted early and give up.

Successful digital acceleration starts slowly. There are steady increments of improvement in processes and delivery along the way. Think of the digital journey as starting out at a crawl, learning to walk, jog, and eventually to run. But unlike a marathon race, there is no finish line because digital acceleration continues as new technologies become available—a concept known as digital maturity.

The Market Leaders Model

Companies that have reached continuous digital maturity did not do so in a day. Instead, they've developed and expanded over time by adding new platforms and technologies, capitalizing on changing market demands to better serve customers, streamlining business execution models, and bolstering bottom lines in the process.

They're still doing so, adopting and adapting new technologies and new platforms to make consumers' and customers' lives easier, again boosting their balance sheets. Continuous digital maturity, after all, is never-ending.

Missed Opportunity

A small New Jersey–based distributing company wanted digital transformation for its end-to-end business. In the beginning, the company embraced the DOM and its leaders were on board with the possibilities of digital. But as the journey continued their enthusiasm waned like so many other companies that come up short of transformation. Two years into implementation—and with 90% of the transformation complete—the company gave up and reverted to its old ways.

The company's executives, with their historically siloed views on how to run the business, ran out of patience. That's common with digital transformation failures because a solid digital road map calls for an integrated ecosystem. That's tough when everyone has a different vision or agenda for the company. The company decided, too, that it didn't have the appetite for enhanced growth that comes with a digital business platform.

Also, as this distribution company realized, the potential of a new platform doesn't suddenly happen on day one. Too many companies think that way. Instead, confidence, patience, and a solid belief in what *can be* play pivotal roles in successful transformation. It's the scenario of learning to crawl first, then walk, jog, and eventually run.

Along the journey there will be failures and changes, shifts and realignments, and new processes and challenges. A company's leaders need to understand up front that digital transformation is a long-haul process—the marathon journey. Like the distribution company, they'll likely hit the wall at least once—just as in a marathon when a runner usually hits the wall around the 20-mile mark. Will you give up like the distributing company? Or will you triumph and finish the marathon strong? It's your choice but be aware that the rewards of a strong finish can be well worth it.

10 Reasons Digital Transformation Fails

1. Failure to accept incremental implementation over an extended period of time.
2. Aversion to risk and a lack of willingness to give up old processes in favor of streamlined new ones.
3. Stakeholders (leaders, too) thinking only about their job function and failing to see the big picture.
4. Executive refusal to relinquish siloed operations and control.
5. Inability of leaders to understand needs versus wants.
6. Lack of widespread training and adoption of new systems.
7. Lack of communication and collaboration, which leads to failure to keep teams informed of what's happening.
8. Unwillingness to accept failures as part of the transformation process.
9. Pursuing the *cheapest* solution rather than the *best* one.
10. Failure to reinforce the vision throughout the transformation.

Toss Peanuts, Attract Monkeys

Companies and their leaders give plenty of excuses for avoiding the digital journey, including lack of affordability or the desire to save money. That's unfortunate because turning away from digital shows a lack of vision for the future.

Saving money isn't always the best approach, even in tough financial times. Instead, leaders need to invest in their businesses, and not just their people and clients, but also in terms of processes and tools. That's incredibly relevant in highly competitive, fast-changing times like today.

A company unwilling to pay top dollar won't get the best talent, either. Paying less money for goods or services also often creates a cheaper product that ends up a bandage as opposed to a solution. That patch could cost more money and take up more resources and time over the long haul.

But there are solutions. Just as every marathon ends with a medal, every transformation milestone means recognition and confidence to achieve the next level on the DOM-in-motion journey to digital maturity.

PATHWAYS TO GROWTH: A ROUNDUP

- The digital operating model—DOM—gives any company of any size or industry the power to transform more lives effectively and efficiently and grow exponentially.
- Disrupt or be disrupted is the mantra and the choice facing businesses today amid changing demographics, consumer demands, and the competition.
- The three must-have elements of the digital operating model are culture—the people mindset to embrace the adoption of new ideas and the speed that digital enables; business platform—the right technology to run business processes; and innovation—the openness to come up with and welcome new technology, ideas, and processes.
- DOM identifies five levels of achievement on the journey to continuous digital maturity. The levels are digital infancy→early experiments→digitally credible→digitally mature→the market leaders.
- Think of a business operating on a platform like a shopping mall— one venue, with many and varied storefronts or options inside. Everything—horizontal functions internally in a business and vertical ones that serve customers—is instantly accessible and connected in one location.
- Digital transformation doesn't happen overnight. It's like a marathon race that takes commitment, thorough assessment, planning, and incremental implementation. Acceleration starts slowly with steady improvement along the way.

CHAPTER 2

DOM in Motion

Do not judge me by my successes, judge me by how many times I fell down and got back up again.[1]

—Nelson Mandela

All businesses are not giants of their industry or even aspire to be. But every business has more possibilities than it realizes and looks for ways to differentiate itself from its competitors.

Disruption on the business side as well as with technology through business platforms can capitalize on that untapped potential, provide more and better services, and at a cost savings with incredible growth potential. DOM is the enabling pathway, that when embraced fully by a company, creates the velocity—DOM in motion—to create a win, win, win situation.

WHY TAKE THE JOURNEY?

For many companies, the onset of the COVID-19 pandemic meant a digital scramble to patch together systems to keep functioning and maintain continuity for customers. Some systems worked better than others.

Many companies faced initial slowdowns; others couldn't meet the challenges and had to shut down. But some saw the potential and disrupted their industries.

DOM Acceleration

Quest Food Management Services is one of those that opted to disrupt. The Lombard, Illinois–based food services group provides services to business, industry, higher education, conference centers, and the K-12 segment in the Midwest, with more than $65 million in annual revenue.

Though the company implemented a food services management software platform prior to the pandemic, adoption was slow and growth only incremental, according to company President Nicholas Saccaro. Then COVID hit and upended everything.

"As we started to reopen from COVID, our operating model completely changed. Instead of opening a cafeteria and serving five hundred kids a lunch period and so on, where we could rely on all this tribal knowledge of existing personnel, now we are doing seven- and fourteen-day meal kits and drive-through distribution where there is absolutely no data, no tribal knowledge to go off of whatsoever," says Saccaro. "So, the adoption of the food management platform in our organization skyrocketed because people found that this was an opportunity to get better data to be able to leverage the learnings and the experiences we were seeing literally every single day."

As Quest accelerated its digital journey—DOM in motion—the company transformed itself. "We were kind of reinventing our model," Saccaro says. "The pandemic really kind of accelerated our adoption and use of these digital tools because it was so important for us to be able to plan the business accordingly. If we weren't able to utilize systems like that where we could forecast production needs or track production trends, we wouldn't know how much to order or how many staffers we had to bring in. It was like starting a new business or a new division of our organization."

The pandemic further shaped people's experiences with food and dining, says Saccaro. Now they utilize technology to be able eat food where they want, when they want, and how they want, and to have access to all kinds of broad options. "This is absolutely going to transform the way we think about customer experience," he adds.

Pre-pandemic Quest was at DOM Level 2/early experimenters—still mired in siloed systems, some operations manual and others automated, many disconnected, and technology hesitant. Then, out of necessity, the company embraced the DOM. Today the company is innovating, has a high-performing culture, and has defined metrics to measure its operations.

In other words, it is a Level 3/digitally credible company on the way to Level 4/digitally mature.

Rethinking Your Space

Now is the time for businesses of all sizes to look toward the future, assess their systems and processes, and rethink the possibilities in their industries. It's time to look to innovative ideas and processes, and rebuild bigger and better.

The traditional linear mindset—one step and one customer at a time—is being replaced with the digital mindset that enables small companies to compete on the same playing field as behemoths.

The business model and business objective remain unchanged; it's the execution phase empowered by an innovative thought process that ultimately enables a shift to a digital culture and DOM in motion. Already, experts predict that companies worldwide will spend close to $7 trillion on digital transformation between 2020 and 2023.[2]

Breakwater Treatment & Wellness is a great example of a company that embraced the digital operating model as a pathway to focus on what makes it unique—its processes. The Cranbury, New Jersey–based cannabis products and services company provides a high-end educational shopping experience to customers, according to Andrew Zaleski, Breakwater's President. All the cannabis buds are hand-trimmed to ensure the highest quality. Plus, the company recruits top-notch cultivation and harvesting experts and is involved in research to continually improve its products.

The power of DOM helps Breakwater measure and maintain its quality products as well as provides a platform to deliver a better experience to customers. "Breakwater is fully committed to this process, which has allowed us to sustain a reputation for high quality over low cost and high-volume alternatives," says Zaleski.

CHANGING DEMOGRAPHICS

For those people and companies not yet convinced that disruption and digital acceleration are essential to survival, consider some of the changes in demographics and consumer behaviors happening today and the expected possibilities for tomorrow. Companies with aspirations to survive and thrive into the next decade will need to respond to the needs and demands of these changing forces.

World population will surpass 8 billion by 2025, according to United Nations projections.[3] Leading markets will shift more to Asia. Millennials and Gen Z have been joined by Generation Alpha and soon a new generation. These generations have brains wired differently than earlier generations and bring new expectations and new skill sets as they join the workforce in ever greater numbers. Asian markets and consumers differ from their Western counterparts, too.

All of this will further affect consumer and customer purchasing behaviors that already have been changed by the pandemic. Better, faster, smoother, more efficient, and integrated operations and transactions on demand are the expected norm. Slowdowns, glitches, and breakdowns simply are no longer acceptable. This new workforce and consumer will reject products and services as well as delivery and payment systems that don't live up to the latest technology and expectations.

To meet these demands, new businesses will emerge. Existing businesses also have the affordable opportunity to compete if they embrace digital acceleration and maximize their potential through the availability of platform approaches.

Purposeful Companies Poised for the Future

Today's workforce—as well as tomorrow's—want a company's strategies to be driven by purpose that in turn creates a thriving culture. Successes are about a purposeful culture and environment pinned on the premise of how to make lives easier. It's no longer only about profits. Digital is about simpler, faster, and better. When companies and people pay attention to that, the profits and the successes follow.

Values Front and Center

If that sounds like a stretch, again look at Quest. When the pandemic hit, Saccaro says, the company decided early on that no matter what happened, the company would remain true to its longtime core values of integrity, responsiveness, accountability, respect, and excellence among its teams, communities, and customers.

"We said we are going to lean on those values," says Saccaro, "even if it means we have to endure some more pain right now to do what we think is right. If we are making decisions that are in alignment with our values, we will find a way to navigate through this."

A few of the ways Quest did that during the pandemic included:

- Taking on a $5 million-plus Paycheck Protection Program (a Small Business Administration–backed loan program) loan to keep employees whole for eight weeks when there was literally nothing for them to do because the schools were shut down.
- Making sure that clients who helped keep their employees financially secure weren't billed while the company received the PPP money so they wouldn't feel like Quest was taking advantage of them.
- Mike McTaggart, Quest's owner, going without a salary so the money could go to food pantries and creating the Quest Cares Fund for employees.

"At every single turn our intentions were to keep our mission, vision, and values front and center and not change who we are," says Saccaro. "It's easy to have solid relationships when things are going well but you really strengthen them and build them over the long haul when things aren't going well."

The company did all that and it "absolutely" paid off, adds Saccaro, in "the commitment we have seen from our clients in terms of the contract extensions, their willingness to be flexible with us, and the new business we've signed. We have had two incredible growth years."

Today's successful leaders like Saccaro understand the value of purpose and people—the right culture.

The Strength of Culture

David Granson also believes in the importance of culture. He is managing director of wealth management for New York–headquartered Goldman Sachs, the global investment banking, securities, and investment management firm. He has been with the company for 25 years. That's a strong testament to the company's culture.

"I believe the majority of professionals aspire for three things in their employment: to learn, to earn a competitive living consistent with individual objectives, and to feel they are making a difference," says Granson. "Based on my criteria, Goldman Sachs is one of the world's great talent networks—not just in finance, but in industry at large—and the firm has afforded me the ability to achieve all three."

Vision

Mastercard is a leader, too, with visionary executives that put people, purpose, and connection at the forefront. The company has a purpose manifesto—"to connect everyone to priceless possibilities." That manifesto touches on responsibility, trust, working together, innovation, and "to let basic human decency serve as our guide."[4]

Former CEO Ajay Banga famously coined the term "decency quotient," or "DQ." That's shorthand for treating others how they would wish to be treated. "Decency," Banga says, "is the foundation for the kinds of relationships that drive respect, innovation, urgency, and enterprise-wide thinking. It's what supports and inspires people to believe that they can trust you, and that you will have your hand on their back, and not in their face. This lets them know that they can bring their full hearts and minds to all that they do."[5]

That kind of culture and vision, which continues now beyond Banga's tenure, has made a difference for millions of people around the world, and for Mastercard.

Goldman Sachs is another company with strong culture and vision. Says Granson, "In my view, a determined professional can be fulfilled and challenged working with outstanding, collaborative, and dedicated colleagues, coupled with tremendous clients in an ever-evolving industry of global importance."

"Effectively, Goldman's well-known 'culture of success' and client-first mindset has been the crux of my experience and my standard of comparison." adds Granson, who is also an adjunct professor at Georgetown University's McDonough School of Business.

EXPLORE/EXPLOIT/DISRUPT

Now let's look closer at the five levels to a full and robust digital operating model and see how a company can evolve as it learns to explore, exploit, and disrupt its industry.

The Journey

Digital transformation is a journey, and the business platform a milestone to measure where a company is on that journey toward continuous innovation and exponential growth as shown in Figure 2.1. Just because a company hasn't yet reached Level 5 of the DOM, though, doesn't mean that it's not on the right path. DOM in motion, after all, creates the velocity necessary for growth.

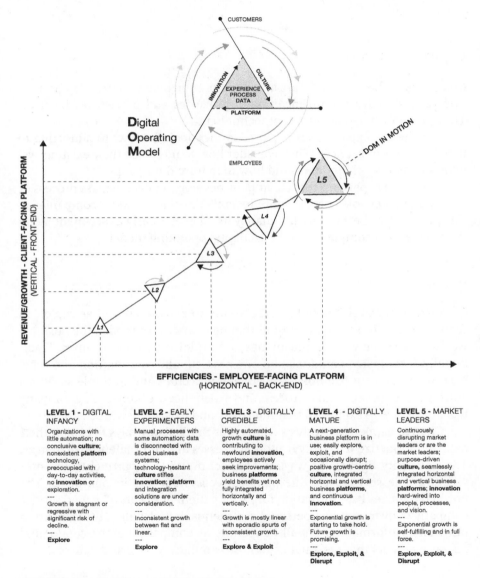

FIGURE 2.1   Digital maturity Levels 1 through 5.

The bigger question is determining a company's current level of digital maturity. That's important because understanding the various maturity levels helps clarify the digital journey and what it will take to reach the next level and, eventually, Level 5—the market leaders. Level 5 companies are ongoing disruptors and grow exponentially as they build purposeful organizations.

Exploration Phase

Companies at Levels 1 and 2 are at the exploration phase on the DOM model. They already have certain meaningful processes and procedures in place. They probably have some form of technology.

But these companies want more, so they look for how to add value to their products or services. They consider how to monetize their existing systems and assets—their data—and how to mature their people.

The result is perhaps that a company develops a new business process or model and its people become more receptive to change. Most companies at this point are at Level 1/digital infancy and Level 2/early experimenters on the journey to a complete and robust digital operating model.

Exploit

Companies at Level 3 now have the ability to explore as well as exploit in their business. To make the most of that new process or model, the business works to leverage what it already has and exploit new opportunities. Traditionally, a company would take on one problem and one solution at a time. Now with platform technology, it's one architecture and multiple solutions and outcomes because data, process, and experience are built in. The company has the chance to exploit all that internally and externally with customers.

Change happens steadily as companies think about ways to exploit their data and monetize it to deliver more processes and, ultimately, experiences. The university figures out ways to connect multiple departments and provide multiple services via one platform ecosystem and in one place. The hospital digitizes its information for faster patient check-in. The food service company delivers not just personalized menus, but also direct-to-consumer nutritional information. It's all happening as companies embrace a digital operating model that personalizes and streamlines service and delivery.

Most companies at this point are at Level 3/digitally credible and Level 4/digitally mature on the journey to a complete and robust digital operating model.

Moving On

IndiaFirst Life Insurance Company Limited is already at Level 3 and moving to Level 4 on the DOM journey with its robust business platform SIMPLIFY, a unified sales app for customer acquisition and servicing. Known as "One Sales Universe," the app enables sales with a seamless flow across all stages of application, from lead to policy conversion to ongoing policy servicing. Apart from enabling 99.5% reduction in paper-based processing, this futuristic application resulted in an approximate 25% reduction in log-in to issuance turnaround time and a 50% reduction in sales queries within three months of launch.

This comprehensive and complete app helped IndiaFirst Life stay nimble and differentiate itself from the competition. As one of the youngest and the fastest-growing life insurance firms in India, IndiaFirst Life continues to innovate to improve in line with its #EmployeeFirst and #CustomerFirst ideologies.

Disrupt Holds the Power

The power of artificial intelligence enables companies to explore and exploit, but not to disrupt. To disrupt—companies at Level 4 and Level 5—requires an understanding of evolving markets and the ability to respond quickly to shifts with the right product or service. Disruption creates the real power of exponential growth. Once a company has explored options and developed new business processes, then leveraged its existing model and assets as part of the exploit phase, the next step is to disrupt.

Disruption is not for everyone. If the milk producer doesn't want to change the milk-producing industry or if a restaurant can't think about change, disruption won't happen. But if the restaurant does want to disrupt, the sky is the limit.

From London to New York to San Francisco, and beyond, food service is happening digitally and with less human interaction at restaurants, in schools, and in hospitals. Digital payments also have become the default method, whether it's a street vendor in Southeast Asia taking payments via mobile phones or a shop owner or service provider in Copenhagen looking to the process to complete transactions.

The rideshare business is another digital platform success. Cars certainly aren't a new form of transportation, and neither is it new or unusual that people want to go from place to place. A little more than a decade ago, rideshare meant hailing a cab or hiring a limousine service. Change meant more competition in the form of another taxi or limo company or perhaps subscription or on-call service.

Then came business platforms that exploited the demand and disrupted the industry. These platforms provided the ecosystem and the opportunity to connect supply and demand, provide more service to consumers—anytime, door-to-door, or cell-phone-to-cell-phone pick-up and delivery—and all with the ability to massively scale up.

Once implemented, that's exactly what has happened. The impossible is possible. Companies at this point are at Level 4/digitally mature and Level 5/ market leaders with continuous digital maturity.

ENTREPRENEURIAL/DIGITAL MINDSET VERSUS LINEAR MINDSET

For this kind of new acceleration to thrive, the linear mindset of the past must give way to the digital mindset. Remember, a digital culture or mindset is one of the three foundational elements of the DOM.

Digital today does not mean grabbing the latest technology as soon as it comes out to try to automate something, then figure out how to make it all function within the status quo. The digital mindset is an intentional approach to identifying challenges and creating innovative solutions through the use of technology as a tool to make lives easier, business experiences better, and data safer, while fueling unimaginable growth in the process.

New Mindset

Many of us grew up with the linear mindset—do one task at a time, complete it, then move on to the next. Operations and thinking were siloed and management top-down. Today's digital mindset is about accomplishing multiple tasks at the same time, agile thinking, collaboration, transparency, and clarity. Authenticity and vulnerability matter.

Customers today want to know a business and its people are authentic. If a person or company says, "I'm the best," people head elsewhere. The digital mindset world dictates that instead they say, "We're working harder to get better every day." Today's consumers listen to the latter and come back. Continuous growth and improvement is the new mantra.

Anything Is Possible

Even old-school businesses can change when they adopt a modern enlightened culture.

Crum & Forster is a diversified specialty insurance company that dates to 1822. Today the Morristown, New Jersey–based insurer is part of Fairfax Financial Holdings Limited, a global insurance and investment management company.

In 2014, C&F had a traditional insurance company culture with a centralized, top-down management style. Results were mediocre and employee satisfaction was low. Marc Adee, C&F's new CEO at the time, and his management team recognized that to grow and thrive in a highly competitive business, they would have to undertake a transformational journey that began with the company's culture.

Fast forward to today, a dramatically changed C&F is a company its employees see as a great place to work, it is increasingly seen as a great business partner, and the company has more than doubled top-line revenue and profit margins since it began its cultural transformation.

DATA OWNERSHIP

With a digital mindset, equally as important as this new transparent approach is ownership of data. That's because in a digital world, as mentioned earlier, data is monetized; it's the commodity.

Equally important is data integrity—the reliability and trustworthiness of the data in a company's control. After all, ownership is control, which in turn can create data trust and encourage return and long-term customers, or the opposite if data isn't protected and used for its stated purpose.

Who Controls It?

Companies can create their own data or they can collect it from others and monetize it. It can be personalized or depersonalized. But collection of that data and whether a company has ownership of the data, and ownership for a specific use even when it's depersonalized, raises more questions.

People—especially younger generations—relinquish de facto control of their data all the time across social media channels. These channels take advantage of that and monetize users' data. Targeted ads based on someone's social media interests are a good example of that.

In some cases, companies depersonalize the data they own. A hospital system could depersonalize data to identify incident trends to determine optimal staffing.

Definitions

Every piece of data on a business platform has what's known as a physical and a logical definition. The physical is the obvious—a name is a name, for example. But take away the name—de-identify it—and the data becomes an ID in the system that can be aggregated to show trends and patterns as in the hospital scenario above. Then it becomes what's known as logical data. Logical data explains how the data is used to solve a specific problem.

Veteran CIO Ian Worden cautions that in the healthcare field, ownership of data as well as for a specific use can be more complex even when it's de-identified. But if a company reaches digital maturity, owns the data, and has developed its own unique data, all that can be monetized, exploited, and markets disrupted for exponential growth.

NETWORK EFFECT/PLATFORM EFFECT

That exponential growth is possible with business platforms in part because of the network or platform effect. That's the reality that platform user numbers snowball as services increase and more users tap into the system.

The up-front expense to build the basic platform could be initially more expensive and take additional time. But once complete, the platform has the capability to easily and quickly scale up, and use grows exponentially.

For example, Whitsons Culinary Group is a New York–based company that provides farm-to-table food management services. Its customers include public school districts and senior living facilities. Founded in 1979, the company used to utilize traditional siloed operations. Then Whitsons CEO Paul Whitcomb decided to disrupt and embrace a digital operating model. For Whitsons, that meant an enterprise resource planning (ERP) solution that included an end-to-end system to track, manage, and deploy food products to its clients.

With its school district clients, for example, what started out as a system utilized by only a few hundred chefs now has tens of thousands of users—the network effect. As part of its digital regeneration, Whitsons introduced a menu-viewing app that offers students, parents, and district staff menu planning, nutrition information, meal ingredients, and real-time allergen information at their fingertips. It's all available via an app on their mobile devices or computers. Giving consumers that kind of personalized service and ease of use led to significant user adoption—the platform effect.

That's disruption; that's transformation; that's exponential growth.

For those who still doubt the power of the platform effect, consider that Apple reportedly has paid developers approximately $260 billion since the App Store launched in 2008. That's no small amount paid out to developers of those apps everyone downloads, usually based on word-of-mouth or e-delivered suggestions from others.[6]

ROI VERSUS THE NEW ROR

The platform effect also has changed how companies look at monetary return in this new digital world. Traditionally, return on investment (ROI) was what mattered. Now, with the power of the business platform, that's being replaced by rate on return (ROR).

With a pre-DOM approach, someone might look at a company experiencing exponential or dramatic growth as an aberration. But in today's digital world it's not. That growth is fast becoming the norm across all types of industries. One of the reasons is a shift in how businesses approach technology purchasing.

Typically, companies looked at technology acquisitions based on ROI—one technology or one application to solve one problem. The goal was to hopefully realize a dollar-for-dollar return on the investment.

Today's disruptive strategy, instead, enables a new and better thinking—investing for multiple returns—ROR. With the digital mindset, businesses don't just want $100 worth of value for $100 spent. Rather they want $1,000 value or even $100,000 value for that initial $100 investment. This ROR is feasible and realistic with disruptive thinking and digital platforms. Think in terms of how Whitsons' platform use snowballed.

Also, the use of business platforms with common assets—the shopping mall analogy from Chapter 1—as well as reusable assets further adds to the value equation. The platform provides the power for multiple outcomes at the same time as opposed to just one with the traditional ROI approach.

WHAT ABOUT THE CLOUD?

When we talk about digital transformation, the elephant in the room is "the Cloud." The Cloud makes it possible. Of course we're not talking about a real cloud—one of those white fluffy marshmallows in the sky. Rather, "the Cloud" is a bank of computer servers somewhere offsite.

Think of the shopping mall analogy from earlier. The first step in constructing the mall is finding the right real estate or location. Translated to digital jargon, that's the Cloud, which helps optimize operational costs and guarantee uptime through its shared real estate and services. Whitsons, for example, counts on the Cloud for its end-to-end business platform.

Business Benefits

Let's look closer at what utilizing Cloud capabilities can mean for a company, its people, processes, and IT operations. Among other things, the Cloud provides business continuity, contingencies, risk mitigation, and faster scalability—a necessity as a company grows.

Some things to consider include:

- How does utilizing the Cloud affect that business?
- How does it affect customers?
- What's left if everything about a business is offsite in the Cloud?

The Cloud is about digital platforms that streamline and expedite a business, its operations, data, and experiences. It's a common sharing platform for the infrastructure of a business. When someone clicks on a function in the Cloud, they're not really selecting one thing. As mentioned earlier, they're actually activating an entire platform ecosystem.

It's not a new concept. Over the past two decades, application service providers have connected businesses to networks via installed internet-based applications. But as work-from-home has become the necessity and the norm, human assets more than ever before have been transferred to the Cloud to coexist with business assets.

Almost by default, this move to digital has created a more fluid, transformative, technological environment, which allows for continuous collaboration, co-creation, and cooperation. Chances are over the past several years or so we've all heard at least once a business leader or manager say some iteration of how working from home could never work, but it really has worked.

Better and Better

For many companies, this model shift to a virtual environment can and has led to improved efficiency, better power of human capabilities, more outcomes from IT systems, and superior customer experiences. This is the power of business connected to the Cloud.

Now imagine the endless possibilities if a company voluntarily makes the move to embrace all the Cloud can offer. That's business platforms as a service (BPaaS). Think of BPaaS, which includes software as a service (SaaS) applications, as delivering end-to-end business services for customers. It's an all-inclusive framework customized to an individual internal and external business's needs and fully digitized for accessibility, scalability, and speed.

This is the ultimate mall, the one-stop shop for all your business needs—your customers' needs as well as the ability to access multiple companies, applications, and services for multi-functionality, and best of all, one investment in the place of 10. Considering the availability of business services and products these days, simplification of this kind will create a more streamlined working environment for all and allow for exponential growth.

PATHWAYS TO GROWTH: A ROUNDUP

- The business model and business objective of this new digital world remain unchanged; it's the execution phase empowered by an innovative thought process that ultimately enables a shift to a digital culture and digital operating model.
- Companies at Levels 1 and 2 are at the exploration phase on the DOM model. Companies at Level 3 now have the ability to explore as well as exploit in their business.
- Disruption creates the real power of exponential growth. To disrupt requires an understanding of evolving markets and the ability to respond quickly to shifts with the right product or service. These are companies at Levels 4 and 5.
- Digital transformation success today is about first and foremost creating a purposeful culture and environment pinned on the premise of how to make lives easier and better. Profits will follow.

- Exponential growth is possible with business platforms in part because of the network or platform effect—the reality that platform user numbers snowball as services increase and more users tap into the system.

- The linear mindset—do one task at a time, complete it, then move on to the next—has been replaced by today's digital mindset. That's about accomplishing multiple tasks at the same time, agile thinking, collaboration, transparency, and clarity. Authenticity and vulnerability also matter.

- Data ownership is crucial today because in a digital world data is the commodity that's monetized.

- Return on investment (ROI) or dollar earned for dollar spent is out. The new mantra with today's business platforms is rate on return, or ROR, which is investing for multiple returns. That's made possible by the platform effect.

CHAPTER 3

The New Normal

As Hindu scripture, the Bhagavad Gita, reminds us, "Due rewards of our actions will reach us in course of time."[1]

Every business takes its own unique path to digital transformation. But all those businesses must share varying versions of the same common denominators: culture, business platform, and innovation.

Ongoing innovation leads to new ways to make consumers' lives easier. The right business platform delivers a good experience, and together they enhance a culture that embraces digital change.

Welcome to the new normal as companies today scramble to remain relevant, to keep up with consumers' evolving needs, and to master the art of customer retention. Those companies that have learned how to do that and grow at the same time create the recipe for exponential growth.

DOM IS A MUST

Every company, no matter its size or industry, from the local food supplier to the national university system, even the corner wine shop, needs all three elements to scale in today's digital economy. The three elements of the DOM don't have to work at the same level; but all must be present to power digital transformation.

Elusive Success

If one element is missing, digital transformation falters. Unfortunately, as mentioned earlier, that happens all too often.

Those failures generally aren't the result of the technology or the platform, but rather the people involved and the execution. That's because execution must be aligned with vision for a business platform to succeed. And, if the stakeholders and leaders—from the bottom to top—aren't on board and in sync, the transformation journey can't succeed.

The People Challenge

No matter the industry or the company, the biggest challenge to digital transformation is people resistant to change. It's not the money or the investment or the time, says Gary McGeddy, President of C&F's Accident and Health division. "It's the resistance of *Homo sapiens* to change."

People tend to like the way things have always been done. The old adage comes to mind, "If it ain't broke, don't fix it." These are the people who don't recognize the power that transformation—including digital—can bring to a company or even its applicability. Years into C&F's transformation and despite growth, there are still people in the company who argue that digital doesn't apply to their business model.

McGeddy's challenge certainly isn't unique (more later on how he's overcoming it). Typically, most companies have some people who aren't open to change or willing to try new approaches no matter how much easier the switch to digital can make their lives or how much benefit to a company, customers, or consumers.

Sometimes, though, as C&F and so many other companies can attest, people can be more receptive to change depending on how the change is implemented. The ancient Indian philosopher, statesman, and teacher Chanakya suggested that when someone eats a plate of hot food, it's best to not begin at the center. Rather, eat the food from the plate's outer edges first and the diner is less likely to burn their mouth on the food.[2]

The same can be said about innovation and change. Innovative complex changes can be implemented incrementally, a little bit at a time—from the outer edges as Chanakya suggests. Instead of massive upheaval and change all at once, introducing and implementing change incrementally often eases the transition and helps overcome resistance. Delivering the innovation on a familiar device, too, like a mobile phone or smart speaker, can make change more palatable and lessen any resentment or challenge to change.

WHEN IT WORKS AND WHEN IT DOESN'T. . .

For some companies, digital transformation is a relatively smooth process. For others, the journey can be bumpy, full of detours and unexpected challenges. Some businesses go the distance; others come up short.

A Tale of Two Businesses

Two Midwestern food management companies at about the same time decided to embrace digital transformation. Both initially believed in the potential of the business platform.

As the starting point on their journeys, each assessed where their company was on the path to digital maturity. One of the businesses had buy-in across the board by its people and stakeholders. The other business ran into Mr./Ms. Negative—individuals with their own personal agendas and not the best interests of the entire company paramount.

The company with the buy-in scored a rousing and successful transformation that doubled and later tripled growth that continues today. The other company's attempts at transformation came up short and the company eventually abandoned its initial goals.

Missing Culture Piece

A university in Leicester, England, wanted to improve on inefficiencies and inconsistencies across IT systems for its more than 20,000 students and staff.[3] The goal was to create a platform that offered a better student experience. That included learning, teaching, research, and business operations across the university's various campuses that existed at the time. Plus, the university wanted a simple framework to move forward.

At the time the university's information technology systems were a decentralized hodgepodge collection of different operations and approaches in various locations. Specifically, the university wanted to integrate those siloed systems so that it could generate a common report to track students in the university system—everything from attendance and finance to library use, learning management, and so on.

That wasn't possible because all the different systems didn't even have a single way of defining how a student's name appeared in the various systems. So, the school's IT department along with its governing board, and with the backing of Steve Butcher, then Head of Procurement and Shared Services for the former Higher Education Funding Council for England, agreed to embrace development and implementation of a new business platform to do all that and more.

The platform was proven successful; the willingness for disruption/ innovation was there. The university even had the funding in place. But the cultural mindset wasn't right. The leaders and stakeholders weren't in sync; among leadership, even one Mr./Ms. Negative can, and in this case did, torpedo the transformation. The people initially involved in the vision weren't part of the attempted execution, and without the original visionaries to follow through with the changeover, the project fizzled.

The concept was ahead of the market, says Paul Hopkins, then chief of the university's IT department and a proponent of the DOM. That was in the early 2010s, when British educators at disparate locations didn't fully grasp the potential of a business platform and weren't ready for the concept of separate yet compatible integrated systems across unique universities.

For new and different ideas to get off the ground, they need to come at the right time, says Hopkins.

Well said.

Another Case of Timing. . .

The timing wasn't right initially for digital transformation at Al Hilal Life either. Said Hathout, CEO of the Bahrain-based life insurance company, first pitched the concept of selling life insurance online to his board of directors in 2018. Traditionally, life insurance relies on in-person sales. In Bahrain, that's typically done in a bank through a bancassurance model where Al Hilal Life agents rely on walk-in bank customers to purchase policies.

Well before the COVID-19 pandemic, Hathout recognized that as more people relied on the internet and digital transactions, the insurance business needed to provide that experience, too, to remain competitive. In addition, as more consumers look to digital banking, that means fewer bank walk-ins and fewer potential insurance policy sales.

Despite all that, Al Hilal Life's overall direction at the time was not aligned with investing in online life insurance sales—an unproven sales model for a line of business that historically relies on face-to-face selling and direct interactions with customers. The timing simply wasn't right.

When It Works

Fast forward two years; COVID-19 grips the world, Bahrain included, and the few walk-ins at banks became scarce. So Hathout as well as the Al Hilal Life board realized this was a life-or-death situation where it was clear that even if Al Hilal Life rides out this pandemic, people will not go back to the old ways, so eventually the company needs to do online sales.

They decided to proceed, and not just with online life insurance sales. Instead, Al Hilal Life's board and management opted to disrupt. That meant offering online personally tailored products with immediate coverage and no in-person meetings.

Al Hilal Life and its technology partners had to not only develop self-service tools, but also leverage the digital platform to generate referrals, the lifeline in life insurance, says Hathout. That meant taking a legacy mindset/culture and transforming it. "Technology was not really the biggest challenge," says Hathout, "It was the learning process. I'm not really a technology nerd. What I learned in the last months is more than my entire life. It's a nice journey to go through, frustrating sometimes, but eventually when you start to see the actual results begin to materialize you find out it is worth it."

When the transformation began only a few people in the company backed Hathout's plan. Today it's a far different story. Nearly everyone in the company changed their mentality when they saw what can be done with digital (the platform effect). "We have made the digital process flawless without any kind of paper, very quick and simple," he says. "We are trying to be the first company in Bahrain with life insurance totally online. Today we have 10% market share of $300 million in U.S. dollars. Tomorrow I hope to grow that market to perhaps 10% of $1 billion by expanding that market."

A Great Idea Hits Snags

LifeNexus Inc. was a company that in 2009 came up with the iChip, a personalized microchip embedded in a plastic card. Just like the bank cards with chipped personal identification information that nearly all of us have now, the concept was for a chipped card that was a key that could be authenticated and connect with someone's personal health data on the Cloud. The thinking was that a person shouldn't have to recall all their health data whenever they visit a healthcare provider or go to a hospital.

Revolutionary at the time, the chip had the ability to disrupt the health-care space. The company and its innovators even had formal Series A funding. Remember, the university in Leicester, England, that had the idea to disrupt its space also had funding, but implementation fizzled? The health-data chip fizzled, too, because rather than embrace the innovation, exploit it, and move forward, the company's leaders tried to make it fit into the existing system. It was the square peg in the round hole stymied by a culture unwilling to disrupt the status quo. The technology was there but the healthcare ecosystem wasn't ready to fully embrace the transformation for a number of reasons, including data privacy concerns.

LifeNexus eventually filed for bankruptcy protection in 2016 and another company, OrangeHook Inc., bought its assets.

Two other similar health information–related platforms—Google Health and Microsoft Health Vault—also didn't take off. However, a third, more recent platform for personalized consumer health records, Apple Health, that works as an app on your iPhone may have a better future.[4]

DIGITAL CULTURE MINDSET

As so many examples in these pages suggest, digital transformation is not just about technology and innovation; it's about a change in the people mindset—the culture—of a company. Leadership as well as employees must openly embrace the change, speed, and agility that digital can enable. Then they can leverage the potential for exponential growth and deliver better experiences for everyone.

New and Better

There's more. Before someone rolls their eyes at the idea of culture as crucial to digital transformation, think again. A solid product or service is no longer enough for customers or consumers.

Customers do business with a company today because of the authenticity and transparency of its people. This is an era that demands openness and a visible mindset. Saying, "I'm the best," doesn't cut it. Continuous growth and improvement—working harder to get better every day—is what counts.

In many companies, the culture is the missing piece. Some people may be stuck in the past and not ready for the change or the speed and fluidity of digital. They could be satisfied with the existing system, no matter how cumbersome or inadequate.

At the university in Leicester, England, the original visionaries were no longer on board and, therefore, couldn't spearhead and promote the new platform model, so the execution came up short and transformation didn't happen. Transformation worked at Al Hilal Life, because the initial champion of digital, Said Hathout, spearheaded the change and a dedicated team of believers made it happen.

Three Elements Aligned

Another United Kingdom–based university was more receptive to welcome the DOM. The University of West London now and into the future "leverages the synergies that technology gives us, says Peter John, Ph.D., UWL Vice Chancellor and Chief Executive.

That wasn't always the case, however. In the early 2010s, the university was a languishing educational institution. At the time, everyone figured it was one of *those* universities that will never really be any good or succeed, says Adrian Ellison, UWL Associate Pro Vice-Chancellor and Chief Information Officer.

Numbers don't lie. In the early 2010s, UWL ranked 122 in The Guardian University Guide. The university now ranks 35th in the 2022 Guardian list.[5] To put those numbers in perspective, there were 164 total universities in the UK in 2019.[6] The university almost doubled its income, too, says Ellison.

What happened to turn the tide? One big contributor was that the university's vice chancellor had the foresight and bold leadership savvy to recognize the potential of technology and leverage the digital platform to usher in change, says Ellison. The vice chancellor made digital a key pillar of strategy. The IT director—Ellison—then and now reports directly to the vice chancellor. That's not traditionally been the norm in business.

Absolute measures of success were established, too. One of those measures is IT performance and includes service delivery to satisfaction levels based on a national metric, says Ellison.

The culture and innovation piece. The results of this essential digital leadership have been stunning. The university completely transformed everything from rebuilding its physical campus to changing the curriculum and how it operates.

It's also about people, culture, and executive-level support, says Ellison. "You can have the best digital leader but if you don't take the people or the organization with you, you will never deliver much."

When Ellison joined UWL in 2012, he says, they wanted to put in a new student business platform—a portal where a student could access everything they needed to help them through their academic journey. It would be a virtual university space where students could connect with others; have a collaboration space to work on projects; track attendance, grades, library use, fees, and so on; attend events; and much more. The goal was to leverage the power of existing technology tools—in this case Microsoft Office 365 and the Cloud—to create a better experience for students.

Stakeholder commitment. With top-level university commitment, the help of an external technology partner, and the buy-in of students, the changeover was a huge success. "One of the things I did was to get our student union involved right from the very beginning," says Ellison. "Getting the user community on board is half the battle."

UWL combined commitment to the right platform with a strong culture, and innovation—leveraging existing tools—for a win, win, win then, now, and into the future.

That early stakeholder buy-in is crucial to the success of any new platform in a business. After all, digital transformation is not about implementing the latest and greatest technology; it's about making people's lives better, easier, and more streamlined.

The Mindset Piece

Are objections by your people or your customers grounded in fact? Even if in a small way, it's important to listen to all the stakeholders who will benefit from the digital platform. Their objections or concerns could deal with people, platform, or innovation. Has your company really thought through its digital journey? What's the primary driver of revenue for your company? Is it internal as in manufacturing a product or providing an on-site service? Or is it external schools and institutions? Do you know the primary driver of customer experience? Do you have a mechanism in place to continuously measure customer satisfaction levels and make necessary improvements? Answering these questions helps a company develop a digital mindset, which is foundational to the DOM journey.

The University of West London had the buy-in of all stakeholders from the vice-chancellor and CEO to the student body and digital transformation succeeded overwhelmingly because its people had the right mindset and were ready for transformation. And it's not over yet. In fact, John and his team are looking to the future and more than just technology. "We can't be the master–servant relationship with technology. It can't be that tech is the master and we serve it. It must be the opposite. Technology must serve the communities, the staff, and there must be buy-in. There was buy-in at the top, but now buy-in has to distribute down in order for us to become the kind of university we want to be—the impact university," says John.

Before transformation, Crum & Forster, like many traditional insurance companies, had a linear or waterfall mindset. Remember, that's sequential operations and completing one task at a time, one application or one operation at a time. But with the switch, things changed, especially the timing.

Decentralization helped to untap the potential of people across the company. What emerged is a culture that enables people to embrace an agile, parallel track–thinking mindset—accelerating C&F's speed to market. (More later on the C&F story.)

This further confirms the importance of the culture element of the DOM—the right people in the right structure can unlock high performance.

Authenticity, Trust, and Transparency

Do you use 20 words or one word to describe and connect with your people? If it's the latter, good for you; you're on your way to the clarity and trust necessary for digital transformation. If 20 words is a better description of how you connect, it may be time to rethink your company's plans on how to compete today.

That's because trust defines today's digital culture. Trust is especially important when digital is the connection and it's not possible for everyone to sit together in a room. The COVID-19 lockdown era of forced trust proved that. Many businesses continued successful operations amid lockdown and even experienced unprecedented growth.

Another widespread workplace revelation of the COVID-19 era is trust equals speed. Instead of dozens of people having to sign off on an action, the circumstances of the lockdown led companies to operate leaner, more agile operations.

The concept of trust equals speed in the workplace certainly isn't new. Some successful companies and their leaders have known about that for years.

Effective Communication

With trust comes transparency and more effective communication, too. Instead of companies holding an all-hands meeting once a year, today's digital-empowered companies look to daily and weekly huddles to keep everyone informed and up to speed to make the very most of processes, time, and efforts. That's clarity.

When work from home became the mandate in 2020, Global Furniture Group USA sent its people home. To stay connected, daily digitally enabled team meetings became the norm. Every manager had his entire team on the Microsoft Teams app every day at 8 a.m., says COO Ari Asher. "You almost say, 'Wow, this is normal.' But that wasn't the case; we never did this before."

"COVID helped us restructure how we interact with teams with the help of digital tools that we continue to benefit from," says Asher. The meetings continue, though they have dropped back to several times a week, he says.

Connectivity today doesn't simply mean everyone is online or has access to the internet; it's about communication, collaboration, and camaraderie. Individuals and teams overcome big challenges by breaking them down into smaller ones and dealing with them one step at a time. All these pieces are part of the digital operating model. We're all connected, and all part of the solutions and innovations that bubble up and make the once thought impossible possible.

During the pandemic, C&F experimented with a variety of methods to stay connected with their people. While their decentralized model and digital platform made the transition to the work-from-home world relatively seamless, the C&F management team wanted to keep people informed during an uncertain time—and make them feel connected even while they were working out of their homes.

One of the more popular communications was a weekly Friday check-in note in which Marc Adee started to keep everyone in the loop with respect to all things COVID. Once Adee ran out of pandemic news, the notes evolved to cover a range of business topics including company results, new ventures, and technical aspects of business or career strategies, and also veered into personal anecdotes. "Most of my stories have some relation to a business theme, but some are just for fun to show that CEOs are regular people, too," says Adee.

"The check-ins kind of accidentally turned out to be a great way for me to connect with employees at all levels," he says. "The pandemic made me realize that we had really optimized our culture around our large offices—and that left some people feeling left out. Now I feel more connected to all of our people."

C&F's successful culture goes beyond technology. Says Adee, "There are scenarios that could interrupt our technology—but even as we consider these as realistic disaster scenarios, I believe we would figure something out. That's just part of our culture. When something throws us for a loop, we'll work out a solution. If we get too stuck in our ways, that's probably not going to be the case."

POD: The Right Internal Systems

Agility is essential for a company to have successful and sustainable exponential growth, especially in today's rapidly evolving digitally demanding world. A POD internal structure provides that.

POD is not an acronym; it's the name of a self-contained business unit with all the required elements to deliver the scale necessary for growth today—self-operating, self-governing, and self-managing. Too often companies with traditional top-down business operating models—especially large companies—can't deal with the demands of scale in today's marketplace.

In other words, instead of the traditional dependent business units like finance, sales, human resources, development, and so on functioning as one big multilayered business unit, PODs operate as empowered minimum viable business units. Each can leverage the business, earn money, and budget and control expenses.

Project beginnings. The POD model began as fluid units to maximize potential of a particular project large or small.[7] But they've broadened and evolved to this new POD model that creates a magnifying glass to easily examine and execute the various elements of your business, and maximize product and services delivery to your customers.

POD also maximizes internal communications so that your employees can commit, collaborate, and communicate effectively. Consider how insurance giant C&F decentralized operations and transformed.

Lego-like building blocks. Think of one POD as one Lego building block and a group of PODs as multiple elements that work together to create a sound structure. Companies today need these small independent units because the world is changing so quickly. Small units can pivot much more quickly than large cumbersome ones, thus reacting to market shifts and demands swiftly, smoothly, and easily.

Unlike a siloed business structure, PODs have freedom and empowerment and the ability to leverage the potential of the company. Each POD is integrated into and can access and utilize the power of the business platform. Each has a playbook that yields the desired outcome when everyone follows the cadence.

Delivering growth. The POD structure is designed for growth tomorrow, especially when combined with a RACI matrix. (RACI is an acronym for Responsible, Accountable, Consulted, and Informed.) A RACI matrix is a charting system that details the *who* and *what* in terms of goals, actions, and responsibilities for project completion. It's designed to cut out confusion, deliver accountability, and improve efficiencies and deliverables.

RACI Simplified

- **Responsible:** Who is required to complete a given task?
- **Accountable:** Who makes the decisions and acts on the task?
- **Consulted:** Who is involved in the decision-making and in specific tasks?
- **Informed:** Who must be updated on decisions and actions?

This intentional workflow mechanism is crucial for companies to maintain the forward momentum of exponential growth without sacrificing data, processes, and experience internally or externally for the customers.

The C&F approach. The aim of decentralization at C&F was to increase innovation, reduce project cycle time, strengthen ownership and accountability, build greater engagement and efficiency, and overall better serve the customer, says Tom Bredahl, President of C&F's Surplus and Specialty division.

By decentralizing as many resources and capabilities as possible, C&F inverted decision-making and ownership of every function possible that heretofore had resided at the corporate level and repositioned them "closer to the ground," says Bredahl, "either within our comprising divisions, or even lower by embedding them within sub-segments within divisions."

"The manifestation of this approach was felt nowhere more acutely than within our digital team. We cut dependencies on our centralized corporate hierarchy for virtually all aspects of our operation save for cyber-security and financial reporting. We shifted from a fairly strict, federalist central bureau to a collection of autonomous division states with only a light layer of coordinating services at the top," he says.

"The impact was immediate and positive," continues Bredahl, "even with the expected hiccups from so drastic a change. Gone were the days of waiting months or years for system or process changes. Divisions built or bought what they needed to best serve their particular need. What about redundant cost? What about consistency and compatibility? Challenges for sure, but less problematic than expected."

"Apart from the improvements in our overall performance and delivery, we experienced an additional change that was impactful yet subtle. Morale greatly improved. The typical relationship strains and challenging attitudes among our hard-working and well-meaning developer corps seemed to dissipate. We became a team more in sync with each other. We were now more interested in achieving shared goals than in self-promotion or casting 'blame' on others for deficiencies. We still have challenges, but we now have an infrastructure that smells like action, with a team eager to tackle any challenge," adds Bredahl.

Such is the power of the POD.

THE BUSINESS PLATFORM

A business platform is the technology to run business processes integrated into one or multiple digital platforms. Forget the traditional siloed business operating model. The platform is about correlated thinking—the shopping mall analogy as a one-stop-shop for all your needs—instead of the typical collection of various systems that can include manual as well as online and software-based operations that are often disparate and dysfunctional.

Experience, Process, Data

In addition to the three components essential to digital transformation, companies must know their customers' and employees' experiences, know the processes in the business, and know their data. And then, know how each of those building blocks relates to the various elements of digital transformation. Know all that and you're on your way to success.

Simplified. That's a lot to know and understand. But it's not quite so complex when you consider experience, data, and process in a different context. Let's say you decide to go out for sushi. You have two choices. One upscale, expensive restaurant a block away to the north costs $200 a person. Another small somewhat hole-in-the-wall spot is a block to the south and costs $20 a person. Both have good sushi, so what's the difference in terms of data, process, and experience? The food is the data; the recipe is the process; and the way the food is presented is the experience.

Upscale high-end restaurant serves one small piece of sushi on a big plate and brings 20 plates one after the other. Every bite of sushi is an experience and a memory artistically presented on the plate. It's how the people serve and greet diners, the ambience, and the total experience. Only the finest ingredients—the data—are used. Every bite is designed and curated. That's called delivering food experience.

Hole-in-the-wall, on the other hand, brings out one big plate with different kinds of sushi piled on it. The sushi is tasty, but it's not the same memorable experience.

Similarly, in terms of a business, you can deliver memorable value to customers with the power of a digital operating model that aligns data, process, and experience, and you can command value-based pricing with that. This DOM approach delivers scalability and value and sets a business on the pathway to exponential growth.

One-Stop Shop

Building your business as a platform enables employees, leadership, and customers access to all their needs in one place.

With a large milk cooperative, for example, everything is in one place on the platform—from reusable, reconfigurable assets to customer information, shipping, production, human resources, pricing, and more. Similarly, your customers have their multiple needs from your business organized for easy access and control in one convenient, accessible location—on the platform.

Whatever the size of a company, when it transforms from siloed, disjointed operations into an integrated platform the business performs more efficiently. It's better positioned to deliver better services—experiences—to a greater number of customers today and into the future without disruption or a complete systems overhaul.

When It Works. . .

A digital platform doesn't have to mean tossing out all of a company's legacy systems, which hold important historical data that can be valuable to data analytics. With the right platform, it's possible to leverage existing systems to bring about faster, digital experiences for customers and consumers without building entirely new systems.

A leading U.S. newspaper needed to streamline its classified and display advertising business. The newspaper already had a strong web presence in some of its operations but no mechanism to leverage the internet for its classified and display advertising. The company and its culture had embraced digital and innovation, but the business platform—the third axis—until now was missing in the advertising realm.

Instead, the newspaper's advertising department relied on processes that combined people manually taking orders for ads over the telephone with technologically varied in-house–developed systems to funnel ads from partner ad agencies to its mainframe system. Management wanted to improve customer and consumer experiences through better processes and data management while still maintaining control over ad content printed in the paper. The solution was a digital operating model that leveraged the internet to generate additional ad revenue and provide users a more do-it-yourself approach.

Now the basic reservation process for display advertising space and ad placement is automated. The advertising material is delivered electronically, interfacing with the newspaper's internal production systems. Also centralized is registration and resolution of billing inquiries while providing the newspaper with contract and historical information—data—that allows better management of its business and its customers. Further enhancing control over its data, the newspaper also now has ad lifecycle management and billing online and provides its customers an online system to buy classified advertising products.

A large U.S. milk cooperative also experienced challenges with its existing system operations. Problems included data accuracy as well as speed, downtime, ticket resolution, and security. Business processes, customer experience, and data management all were affected.

So, to enhance its processes, customer experience, and make the most use of its data, the company chose to embrace the DOM and a new Cloud-based digital platform. With its implementation, the cooperative cut costs by 25%; resolved complaints 30% faster; provided 99% system uptime, and enhanced the company's data by offering easy access to system monitoring. And more good news: the new business platform also incorporated existing applications and infrastructure for additional cost savings.

Digital Drives Diversity

The right business platform makes a difference in the nonprofit realm, too. The National GEM Consortium (Graduate Degrees for Minorities in Engineering and Science, Inc.) opted to embrace a DOM and saw growth hit new levels. Founded in 1976, the group's GEM Fellowship program promotes participation of underrepresented minorities in post-graduate applied science, technology, and engineering education.

STEM training. A big reason for lack of minorities in the STEM (Science, Technology, Engineering, and Math) workforce goes back to the common belief that the talent wasn't available or, if it was out there, employers say they couldn't find the talent, says Brennon Marcano, GEM CEO. The consortium helps find and place minority talent in advanced learning programs. With the help of business platform technology—DOM—it's also developing a database that employers can turn to for access to talent.

Companies must validate recruitment costs, especially at a time when money is tight and programs like diversity often are the first to suffer cutbacks. The business platform enables transactional activity—data—to be turned into knowledge so that it can be readily available and preemptive.

"We have been producing the best and the brightest talent who happen to be diverse as well," says Marcano. Now, we take away the logistical excuses companies use—claims they can't find diverse talent—so that an employer simply logs into the business platform, lists its needs, and can access the database of qualified talent. "We always had the talent; where we struggled was with demand and a lack of awareness of the talent."

Before the DOM, just accessing GEM's content online was cumbersome and confusing for potential fellowship applicants as well as employers that sought qualified job candidates. For example, a student who wanted to fill out a fellowship application had to click on 13 different screens.

After implementing a new platform—what Marcano refers to as GEM 2.0—access is streamlined and convenient for students as well as employers. Already the DOM has helped GEM triple in size over the past five years, placing nearly 500 students and working with 128 universities and 60 corporate partners, he says.

Supersize for the future. Marcano has big plans to supersize the program in the future, too. He would like the database to become an aggregator of talent. There's no reason why technology can't drive the challenge of diversity. "We can do it on a small scale, so why not a larger version—perhaps on National Science Foundation level."

He envisions making use of data science capabilities and to develop this supersized centralized database of GEM's 40 years of the best and brightest alumni that, again, happen to be diverse. The business platform will enable an employer to list its needs and instantly be matched up with qualified candidates. Instead of just one candidate, they will be able to access a list of qualified candidates with diversity. It's a win, win, win for all parties.

A platform that can connect education with minorities and companies with diverse talent actually minimizes the divide between the privileged and those who are not in all countries. It delivers access and makes equality possible. The digital operating model is not just for the privileged. It's for everyone.

Built-in Road Map

With a business platform in place, a company, like the nonprofit GEM, also has a built-in road map for the future. As markets dictate the need for a shift/upgrade in operations or delivery of product and services, it's plug and play—or unplug and move on—with new services and systems. That's as opposed to the traditional approach that usually required purchasing new software or systems and hoping they could be configured to work with the existing systems. (Often, they weren't compatible.)

Instead, the new application or software is simply added to the digital platform; all things connect smoothly without service interruptions and in the right order. That instant and across-the-board capability is especially valuable when team members are in varying locations and a work-from-home scenario. A company doesn't have to worry if everyone is on board and whether the changes will be smooth.

With the digital road map, the possibilities are endless. It's a continuous maturity model in which a company with the right platform or platforms sets new goals, achieves them, and does it again and again, all with the same scalable platform.

Amid the COVID-19 lockdown, a local, primarily in-person New York–based copy shop struggled to survive. With a minimal, not always reliable online presence, the company's future seemed bleak. But then its owner woke up to the business potential of the right digital operating model. Embracing a digital platform that could deliver quality copies, enhanced customer experiences, and dependable service online turned the economic tables for the company. In just one year, the company's business soared 40% above pre-pandemic levels.

Intelligent Platform

As the copy shop, GEM Consortium, Al Hilal Life, and so many others found out, the digital operating model offers a bonus. Data is the foundation of intelligence, and when combined with process fluidity and an ability to cater to different types of customers, the three can work together as an intelligent platform. Then a business can utilize high-powered analytics to help predict outcomes and prevent slipups, misinformation, and misdirection.

That means, among other things, a more scientific and less error-prone approach to purchasing, product or service promotions, product design, upgrades, product and service tracking, staffing, customer relationship management, and human resource functions.

Imagine the cost savings for a business with more consistent and accurate ordering and supply purchases, staffing to meet real needs as opposed to estimated needs, and consumer-based design instead of only thinking something might be a good idea. And compare that precision growth, change, marketing, and development to what's happening with the competition. Most likely they're busy reacting to market needs and product design changes. Digital platforms provide the competitive edge.

Changing Processes, Too

A part of Al Hilal Life's rapid digital transformation success lies in the company and its people's relatively quick understanding that rigidity and siloed processes don't directly translate into the business platform model. In other words, the business side of things was ready for the technology and transformation.

"I have learned to let go of a lot of things," says Said Hathout. "Simplicity is the key. We are not putting our current processes into digital; it's not copy and paste. This is not the purpose of the digital transformation. We came up with new processes."

Those new processes powered by a digital platform ecosystem are working. Hathout says the company projects about a 15% increase in sales with the digital operating model. More importantly, the referral impact of digital data mining is huge. Whereas today the company may get 100 referrals via traditional channels, with the digital platform and tools those numbers rise to 200 to 300 referrals, says Hathout.

In the past, he says, referrals meant an Excel spreadsheet with 5,000 to 6,000 names and no one would accurately know the outcomes of those referrals and whether they were properly targeted. "Today with our lead management software, we can distribute those leads and properly track outcomes. We can mine the outcomes and expand targeted marketing."

Endless Possibilities

Platform technology also has the scalability to allow the exponential growth necessary today to disrupt and dominate markets. Whitsons Culinary Group, the New York–based food service management company, took the end-to-end business platform approach and transformed its operations and its business.

Once a hodgepodge of operations that mixed manual and digital functions, today Whitsons is a streamlined 100% digital operating model. That move allowed the company to dramatically increase the number of customers it serves while maintaining the same number of employees. To scale like that without the platform, Whitsons would have had to double the size of its workforce. Not only is the switch a huge cost savings, but a robust digital platform also enables the company to offer more and better services for its customers.

Additionally, the change in the company's business model has a positive societal impact. Thanks to enhanced digital data management, consumers can get a clear understanding of the nutritional value of various foods their clients offer that can lead to better eating habits. As mentioned earlier, Whitsons now has a mobile application that empowers parents to select their children's daily meals with full nutritional value information in mind. This product guarantees customized choices for children's school meals, with the opportunity to contribute to healthier families.

Fluidity

Like Whitsons, businesses today also must be nimble and able to change direction quickly as markets dictate to maintain a competitive advantage. With Cloud accessibility available via platform, it's simple to add a new capability, delete something old, or upgrade to the latest and greatest, whatever and whenever it's needed and all without disruptions to the existing system or massive expenses.

Think of the Cloud as an internet-enabled repository of information, operations, and systems that can help your business run more smoothly, keep your customers happier, and help your employees work smarter. A platform that's Cloud-ready doesn't compromise your data or your business; it sets the stage for efficiencies and growth.

Without Cloud platform readiness, be prepared to be disrupted by your competition.

INNOVATION

The third element of the triangle necessary for digital transformation is innovation. Your people must be open to new ideas and the use of new technologies and processes. They must be excited for change and willing to trade old habits for something new and better.

Risk and Failures

Taking risks and accepting failures is essential. In fact, innovation is built on the ability to fail fast because the failures foster creativity and can lead to new solutions to old and new challenges. In other words, the goal is to quickly determine if an idea holds value without burning an extraordinary amount of money or time.

Those people who quit after one or two misses—or more—aren't ready for innovation. Those who persist, who use knowledge and experience to overcome failures, are the great innovators.

Accepting mistakes, learning from them, and moving on is one of the requisite ingredients within the intentionality formula for creating a culture of success, says David Granson of Goldman Sachs. That's why, he says, he tries to foster a blameless culture. "We know mistakes will be made, but if we don't learn from mistakes, continuously dwell on them, and instead wag a finger at someone, we'll never get their mind. They'll never learn to always be intellectually curious. They will be afraid to dig deeper and you can't let that fester in a team either because the world is too competitive."

Consider that prolific inventor Thomas Edison said of his failed attempts, "I have not failed 10,000 times; I've successfully found 10,000 ways that will not work."[8]

If Edison's optimism doesn't sway those who doubt the importance of failure on the path to innovation, consider that long before *Apple* became a household word, its co-founder Steve Wozniak five times offered his employer Hewlett–Packard his first computer design. That design eventually became the Apple 1 personal computer.[9]

Attitude and Approach

Apparently, H–P at the time wasn't ready for the innovation. When is a company ready? At least when we're talking about digital transformation, the answer stems from what digital is all about—speed.

If it still takes your people 10 days to complete a process, your company isn't ready for digital. But, if your teams continually generate new ideas, suggest new innovations, and take lots less time to do the same job than last week, last month, or last year, they're becoming digitally savvy and ready for the advantages, new experiences, and exponential growth that digital can offer.

Innovation Lab

Innovation is all about ideas—some good, some not so good, and some absolutely great on paper until reality sets in. In tech jargon, it's known as ideation. For many companies, the abundance of so much innovation is happening around them so fast that it's all overwhelming. No one knows where to start in terms of digital change so nothing happens.

Safe place for thought. A great way for a company of any size to avoid overwhelming employees and foster innovation is to create an innovation lab—a place or space where people can try, trade, and develop new ideas quickly. An innovation lab can be about more than technology, too. It's about process innovation as well.

Here are a few solid tips to foster a positive environment:

- Leave the emotion out of the ideas.
- Stay unattached to those ideas.
- Keep moving forward.

Also essential are time limits on ideas—perhaps one to four weeks to develop an idea. In the jargon, that's a maximum of two sprints—one sprint equals two weeks. Build the concept, try it fast, and if it doesn't work, forget it, and move on. If something takes longer, it's no longer an idea; it's a project. Ideas are just that; projects have a beginning and an end.

That's what IndiaFirst Life was doing more than a decade ago at its own technology innovation lab—the Octopus Room. It was staffed by bright young minds tasked with developing new ideas and new ways of doing things, according to Vishakha R M, now the company's Managing Director and CEO. Anything that didn't produce quick results was dropped and the teams moved on to something else.

Driving ideation. Think of an innovation lab as a microcosm of innovation in a specific environment intent on driving ideation. It's a place where people collaborate and provoke thinking that generates a pipeline of ideas and seeds of ideas. One long-time innovation expert describes what happens with ideas in an innovation lab as like throwing darts at a wall and seeing which stick. Not every idea is suited for innovation.

Innovation teams should be small and made up of people focused on innovation and agility, and who understand the model for action. A company's culture needs to promote this kind of creative thinking.

You don't know yet what you don't know. In other words, if a company doesn't have the right data, it can't know what's missing. In the absence of the right data, rather than try to exploit existing systems, companies need to look to outside data and new ideas to implement change.

The capability to analyze and deliver clear and current data is yet another reason why business platforms are so essential in our fast-shifting business environment today.

Formal programs. Innovation is an important element in the DOM model for the future of business. Many small and mid-size companies rush to launch new and innovative ideas on their own. In contrast, big companies create innovation labs or promote entrepreneurship programs with different channels.

Companies including Mastercard and Comcast NBC Universal have formal programs to encourage innovative ideas and businesses. Mastercard's Start Path is a global startup engagement program that helps innovative, fintech later-stage startups scale. The program has been around since 2014 and helped more than 250 startups. New in 2021 is a version of Start Path dedicated to helping companies in the cryptocurrency and blockchain space,[10] and Strive, a program from Mastercard's Center for Inclusive Growth, which is designed to support micro and small businesses to digitize.[11]

Comcast's formal incubator program is The Farm. In essence, it's an innovation lab where groups of young companies have a set period of time to work on ideas. At the end of the mentorship, Comcast may invest in some of the companies.

Plenty of other companies, economic development agencies, and public and private organizations as well offer formal business incubators. Whatever the program, however, always thoroughly research it first before getting involved.

POV versus POC

Also important to the innovation process is the pursuit of proof of value (POV) rather than the more formal proof of concept (POC). Proof of concept simply shows whether or not a proposed idea, approach, product, or whatever actually performs as promised. We don't see if the concept will succeed or fail when implemented in a business.

Proof of value, on the other hand, determines whether an idea, approach, or product actually delivers value in the context of a real business setting—how it can improve a product or process in the real world, for example. We see real working solutions with real business data and processes.

Let's say the new idea is about delivering faster and better customer service as measured by the time it takes to answer a call. If a company averages 90 seconds to answer a call, that means with POC, a call answered in 60 seconds is a win. But POV involves identifying the actual benefits to the customer and in turn the company. For example, even though a call was answered quicker, was the customer satisfied with the solution?

Minimum Viable Concept

Also important in the innovation process is the idea of putting together a minimum viable product that is then tested on a limited basis—what's known as a sandbox environment—using real company data and real problems. Then, based on feedback, the idea or proposed solution is either scraped or further refined and developed before a formal rollout.

For example, when Quest Foods wanted to buy a culinary digital back-end platform, they evaluated various products, selected one, and then had the product vendor test it in this sandbox environment. Within a limited environment, Quest's real users tested the product customized with Quest's data and its rules and regulations to determine how well it operated within the company's system. It wasn't simply a product demonstration; it was about seeing how well the product worked within an end-to-end lifecycle of the business.

ONE STEP AT A TIME

Conversion to a digital operating model, remember, is a journey, not a sprint. When insurance giant Crum & Forster opted to embrace digital, the company was mired in traditional systems and processes.

But as Gary McGeddy of C&F's Accident and Health division explains, the company understood that digital was a very clear necessity to outpace the competition. But the company also recognized that transformational change doesn't happen overnight. So they started incrementally, focusing on the critical areas first, adds McGeddy, those processes that were the most impactful.

Digitalization is no longer *the future*; it's table stakes, says McGeddy. "Our digital initiatives improve our customer experience and differentiate us in the market—in addition to driving our bottom line."

"Insurance is a data and information intensive industry," says John Binder, President of C&F's Commercial Lines division. "We work with billions of data points on a daily basis. It is a minimum baseline requirement to have a robust automation, data management, and business intelligence framework. Those who do not will not last."

PEOPLE OPERATING DIGITALLY

Comparing the sushi experience mentioned earlier with your business highlights the importance of establishing a relationship between high-quality data, well-designed process, and excellent customer experience. The result is People Operating Digitally—the execution of digital transformation.

After all, it's this execution phase that empowers the digital thought process and ultimately creates the cultural shift.

A New Approach

Doing business today is different than in the past. Before digital became the norm, business strategies called for identifying markets and customers or what product offerings provided the greatest bottom-line benefit. Even a business's discussions about its culture were structured and based on the bottom line.

Now, with less physical and more virtual interaction in terms of people and markets, the hybrid model of the work environment, and the changing dynamics of the workforce, company strategies and cultures must change, too. That means, as mentioned, less compartmentalized operations, more transparency and clarity, heightened communications, and greater agility. Today's strategies must be linked with the customer's digital experience and culture must be aligned with the agile mindset.

Execution eats strategy for lunch.

That's the new mantra in our growing digital environment. If a company's structure isn't robust, its strategies go nowhere. A robust structure marries digital systems into a platform or platforms that in turn gives clarity, transparency, and direction for a complete and clear view of a business and its operations. The entire business process is mapped into the platform with execution driven by data and KPI (key performance indicators) metrics.

Fluidity

The DOM provides the platform as well as the fluidity necessary to excel in today's competitive environment in which customers and markets change constantly. Businesses must have the capability to adapt to survive.

Think of a business today in terms of an amoeba—a self-contained organism that continues to change shape as it moves forward. With a platform ecosystem in place, a business can easily adapt its processes. It's plug and play with minimal effort moving forward. Like the amoeba, change becomes smooth and efficient.

Before you think that's a stretch, consider these shape-shifting examples. Lodging was a thriving industry with different hotel chains as well as condo/house lodging options. All coexisted. But then Airbnb took off and disrupted the industry. Lodging companies had two choices: do nothing or react. Some chose the latter, expanded partnerships with other hotels and resort chains, and created their own versions of Airbnb.

Or look at taxi companies in major metropolitan areas. Rideshare companies that utilize Cloud-sharing platform technologies disrupted the industry. Suddenly, curbside pickup, door-to-door service, and instant access took on new meaning in transportation. Now it's no longer enough for the taxis that are left to drive the streets looking for fares or wait for the telephone calls. Taxi services must change shape and adapt their services to meet consumer demand and move forward or disappear.

RULES OF ENGAGEMENT

Some lodging chains and a few transportation companies recognize the importance of having the capability to disrupt, or at the very least, react to disruptions in their industries. They understand the importance of data, knowing that operations/processes must be fluid enough to enable strategy shifts as markets and consumer experiences dictate. And they know that a DOM can help them do all that.

In today's rapidly accelerating digital world, business users can't always differentiate between what they need versus what they want. A DOM helps companies better understand customer behaviors and needs as part of evolving markets and customer experiences, and shift accordingly. It's lean, agile, and about speed. That's compared with more traditional thinking that dictates simply pushing existing products and services.

With the design-thinking approach, a company starts with a prototype limited pilot or test of a process, product, or service—the minimum viable product (MVP) in the sandbox mentioned earlier. Then, if that proves successful, a full rollout is possible. If not, the company moves on to something else. This approach offers businesses the agility necessary to deliver on demand. Hence, design thinking delivers fluidity against the more traditional rigidity.

When design thinking marries with digitally enabled and enhanced data, disruption is feasible. Then, with the POD model—the approach to internal operations mentioned earlier—a company is ready to deliver what its customers need versus what they want.

PATHWAYS TO GROWTH: A ROUNDUP

- Every business takes its own unique path to digital maturity but every successful transformation requires a business have the same three common denominators of a DOM: culture, platform, and innovation.

- If the transformation journey fails, it's usually not because of the technology or platform. Rather it's the people involved and the execution. Not only are people resistant to change, but when the transformation process isn't done right, it likely will fail.

- Taking risks, accepting failures, and learning from them are part of the process. Innovation is built on the ability to fail fast because the failures foster creativity and can lead to new solutions to old and new challenges.

- A company must pay attention to its business operating model. A POD internal structure provides that. *POD* is not an acronym; it's a self-contained business unit with all the required elements to deliver the scale necessary for growth today: self-operating, self-governing, and self-managing.
- Rigidity and siloed processes don't directly translate onto the business platform.
- A digital operating model offers simplicity of process, interconnectivity in experience, and the on-demand access and ability to manipulate data.
- Businesses must learn to differentiate between what they need versus what they want. A DOM utilizes design thinking to better bridge that gap by understanding customer behaviors and needs as part of evolving markets and customer experiences.

CHAPTER 4

DOM in Motion/Small-to-Midsize Company

Food Service Management: Whitsons Culinary Group

DOM bridges the gap—what you want versus what you need.

Level 3 moving toward Level 4 Digital Maturity

Culture: Customers and employees have adopted the business platform.

Platform: Fully automated, integrated business platform ecosystem.

Innovation: Embraced an end-to-end food management system that created the platform effect, brought in new customers, and expanded markets.

The year is 2010. Commercial food services provider Whitsons Culinary Group slowly edges toward digital. Some of its financial and customer relationship management processes and even elements of nutritional analysis utilize isolated digital solutions. But core business processes remain manual and cumbersome.

The company's various systems don't talk to each other and require a person to sign in separately to each one. Excel spreadsheets dominate tracking of farm-to-fork commodities as the company services dozens of public schools across six eastern U.S. states.

At this point Whitsons is at Level 2: Early Experiments in the digital operating model. (Plenty of companies are still there today.)

UPENDED

Then the school food services industry is upended. The Healthy Hunger-Free Kids Act of 2010 is passed by the U.S. Congress and signed into law by President Barack Obama. The law mandates new and upgraded nutrition standards for school lunches.[1]

Daunting Demands

Overnight, new rules apply to school lunches stipulating new counts for calories, sodium, and fats in every meal. Naturally, thousands of school lunches across the country fail to pass muster. Whitsons, with its mishmash of systems—like many other companies on the early digital journey—was underprepared to act fast.

As Whitsons quickly found out, in today's world, rapid change can come from any direction and at any time. At critical moments of change—as happened in 2010—companies must be able to pivot and act fast. That's yet another reason a DOM makes so much sense.

Suddenly, Whitsons clients across the board needed new menus. Each school's lunch program had to be assessed on an individual basis for nutritional content as well as new menus created based on myriad other factors, including:

- What foods could be sourced locally or nationally?
- What inventory already was available in warehouses?
- What to do about limited shelf life for existing inventories?
- How to factor in popular items in particular schools?

Adding to the chaos, each decision required a registered dietitian to dictate which foods and in what quantity were needed to abide by the new guidelines. Then, each needed to be cost out per plate using spreadsheet data from multiple locations. That was a monumental challenge for Whitsons because financial data among locations was kept in silos, making the process cumbersome and labor-intensive.

Tipping Point

Most people think of school lunches as something simple and easy like chicken nuggets and French fries or pizza and chips. The reality, however, is that they're hypercomplex.

Every school lunch is subject to regulatory compliance and nutritional requirements. Companies providing the lunches also have fiduciary and financial responsibilities because, says Whitsons CEO Paul Whitcomb, in a way they're managing money that belongs to various school districts. All this requires specialized skills ranging from nutrition, management, and finance to public relations related to interfacing with schools, communities, and school boards. To address all those different aspects requires a superhuman effort, he adds.

"We knew our legacy software wasn't meeting our needs," says Whitsons CFO Beth Bunster. "It couldn't adequately support our business because various systems didn't talk to each other, double and triple information entry was required, and none of the electronic data linked with accounting. The company didn't even have real-time access to information. Instead, data already was old and outdated by weeks and even a month or more by the time it was received. Those kinds of delays may have been acceptable early in the company, but as Whitsons started to grow, so did the need for timely data and reports. Our real goal was real-time information to act on for the business."

The problem was exacerbated by schools' summer recess, which included cafeteria staff. That meant the September blues—catch up and relearning—for students as well as cafeteria workers. And until the workers relearned the systems, Whitsons as the food service provider would spill money. The trouble, though, was because no real-time information was available until after the fact, it was impossible to identify the exact problem points in the chain.

Today's and Tomorrow's Journey

Whitsons quickly realized there had to be a better way to orchestrate its business. That meant a shift in the company's culture mindset. Siloed legacy thinking was out, replaced by an openness to the digitally savvy platform experience.

To begin the digital journey, the company first had to clearly analyze and thoroughly understand two fundamental factors on the business side and then the same on the technology side: how Whitsons' business processes were set up today and how the company wanted the business to operate in the future—*As Is* and *To Be*. This assessment then formed the foundation to create a company mindset that aligns strategy and execution into the same road map.

Bumps in the Road

Whitsons' assessment began by drawing an end-to-end map of the business and its existing processes. Sounds simple enough. But it turned out that no one at Whitsons had a full vision of where its products and processes started and ended, and there was no company-wide vision for the future.

That disconnect isn't uncommon in all kinds and sizes of companies. Often people don't have a common alignment for the future because they don't have a clear vision of the business end to end. Without that vision it's tough to know what you want or where you're going. Instead, it's business as usual to get by. That doesn't cut it in today's disrupt or be disrupted world.

Adding to the complexities, Whitsons is in food service delivery to schools and senior facilities and must deal with hypercomplex regulatory requirements and fiduciary responsibilities required with any system, says Whitcomb. Plus, he says, the company wanted to build things like nutritional components into their new system so someone didn't have to be a registered dietician to create a healthy menu.

WITH THE FUTURE IN MIND

The family-owned company spent eight months in discussions to figure out what the future Whitsons should look like. With that vision in mind, it could then build an effective business process map.

Agility a Goal

The Whitsons team put together an incremental, purpose-driven approach that aimed for agility. Administrative, operational, and food production activities combined in one unified system that allowed them complete and real-time visibility of all their food service operations.

This time, instead of stitching together a bunch of independent systems that solved small problems in isolation, they committed to the platform mentality of establishing a digitally enabled ecosystem for business-critical functions of the catering model—the shopping mall platform concept (Figure 4.1).

Initially, this included purchase ordering, inventory tracking and distribution, food safety compliance checks, recipe and menu creation, and food preparation. Utilizing a platform approach meant each part could be built and integrated with each other and any existing legacy systems without being dependent on each other. Checks and balances were built into the system, too, to help free on-site managers from some of the tedious day-to-day monitoring that was required.

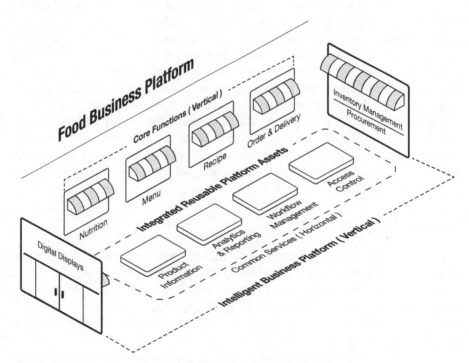

FIGURE 4.1 Build food business platforms like a shopping mall.

Once the infrastructure was in place, new locations, users, and changes could be rolled out across any part of any one of its facilities, without disrupting any other part of the ecosystem. And best of all, any future disruptions—including something as widespread as new nutrition requirements as happened in 2010—can be added smoothly and quickly.

As an aside, that initial digital platform and road map became a powerful digital strategy that gave birth to a disruptive idea/platform—Culinary

Suite—for other companies. That platform digitizes and integrates the back- and front-end processes of the food management business. Backend processes include warehousing, purchasing, inventory, menus, recipes, and nutrition. Front-end processes include digital signage, menu ordering, payment, and delivery. Already, this platform-based experience has been used successfully by more than 100 other companies.

Operational Excellence

Whitsons grew from serving 78 school districts in 2010 to 125 in 2021.With the power of a business platform the company calls DineCentral, recipes are easily created and supported by real-time data on nutritional and allergen content and information on current inventory across locations. Once new meals are chosen, they're sent instantly to a menu management tool. The tool auto-tags menu items with nutritional icons that can be published instantly to a mobile ordering app that parents use to preorder their kids' meals.

With both horizontal and vertical processes integrated and supported by intelligent digital automation, Whitsons now has reclaimed the time that used to be lost on manual processes and can focus on innovating in its field, utilizing its workforce to its maximum potential, and, thus, creating a more fulfilled and empowered workforce.

Speed of Digital

The incremental transformation of Whitsons' core systems to digital took three years to roll out. But the subsequent mobile ordering platform that came next took just three months and was rolled out near-instantly across all their locations, with its popularity quickly growing thanks to the platform effect. Remember, that's when user numbers snowball as services increase and more users tap into the system.

This also shows the exponential rate of exploration and execution that can be attained once the key elements of the DOM become a central part of a business's culture. Not all manual operations were eliminated. Some price and other updates still are done manually but instead of having to be entered multiple times, it's once and then the changes are proliferated across the system.

To put the time savings in more perspective, Whitsons oversees approximately 800 physical locations with teams in every location. That translates to receiving and processing about 10,000 invoices a week. Handling that much data manually would be a tortuous and laborious process. The digital platform does it all automatically, quickly, and accurately.

Says Paul Whitcomb, "The digital journey has definitely been transformative in terms of the availability of and transparency of information and data. The DOM takes away the complexities and allows functionality that our competitors didn't have when we started. We have tighter financial control when it comes to managing inventories and planning, too."

Such is the power of the digital operating model and its ability to deliver better experience.

NEW CHALLENGES

Whitsons continues its success story. With the COVID-19 pandemic, Whitsons faced the challenge head-on backed by its sound digital operating model and came away a winner. And, the company doubled its size in terms of revenue in just 10 years.

Leading the Pack

Today the company is soundly at Level 4/digital maturity on its DOM journey and, if the momentum continues, it will move toward Level 5/market leaders. In a pandemic year of decline for some of the biggest names in the food service industry, Whitsons was named one of the Top 9 fastest-growing food management companies in 2021 by *Food Management* magazine, an industry publication. Additionally, it ranked number 16 on the group's Top 50 list, as well as number 6 in its K–12 group.[2]

That's a testament to the company's ability to adjust rapidly to supply chain disruption and restructuring, changes in menus, and constant fluctuation of school openings and demand. For example, to maintain its leading role in food service management for K–12 during the pandemic, the company used strategies like grab-and-go kiosks dispensing breakfast/lunch bundles, home delivery of meals, multiday breakfast/lunch meal packs for virtual learners and "Take & Bake" meals for weekends and holiday breaks.[3]

What's Ahead?

The company's future is about more and better—that's in terms of business platform (data, process, and experience) for its teams, its customers, and its customers' customers.

"Our data is unique," says Whitcomb, because due to privacy and other issues, the company doesn't own or track its user data. The company does, however, have unidentifiable usage data, purchasing data, and production data available through the platform. Perhaps down the road Whitsons will determine how it can leverage that data to do more than deliver better experiences.

Build versus Buy versus Rent

In today's world and into the future, when a company puts together a digital ecosystem, it usually doesn't build everything from scratch. Rather, companies like Whitsons buy certain other platforms—often SaaS (software as a service on the Cloud)—that are readily available. Whitsons, for example, built its core Dine Central food management platform, but purchased already-built software platforms like meal ordering and digital signage.

With the power of the platform combined with API, all parts connect and work together smoothly as one ecosystem.

Innovation

Innovation at the company is up, and from the bottom up, too, from users of the system. All kinds of people offer new ideas and requests for new features on the platform. For the company, the challenge is to determine the best way to identify and implement the best ideas.

The impossible is possible, but in what order and when are the questions. Whitcomb points to the need to add more definition to the innovation process. "It's been such a backlog because we've never sought out innovation before. Now we need to work on innovation into the future."

ADVICE FOR OTHERS ON THE DOM JOURNEY

Run, don't walk, when it comes to getting started on the digital journey is the consensus. The beginning of the journey may be tough, but once the benefits of a digital operating model become apparent, so will the necessity to do the transformation and do it quickly.

A company can't really afford not to embrace digital. The reason, says Whitsons CFO Bunster, in part stems from all the data made possible and available with the DOM. "You don't know how much money you're wasting because you don't have access to the real-time, accurate data available through the DOM. Forget manual hours saved, it's the data. When you have it, you can turn the ship around before it's too late."

It's that *you don't know what you don't know* and a company really doesn't until the digital operating model opens the door. A business and its leaders don't necessarily need to be smart to be ready for the future. They just need to be able to look at the business and understand what the next evolution will be. The DOM can do the rest.

A Detailed Look at the DOM Journey

COMPANY: Whitsons Culinary Group

INDUSTRY: Food services provider to consumers and public and private organizations including schools, residential and healthcare dining, prepared meals, corporate dining, vending services, and emergency dining.

HEADQUARTERS: Islandia, New York

NUMBER OF EMPLOYEES: approximately 3,000

OBJECTIVES OF ASSESSMENT:

IT alignment with business

- Enhance the return on investment and value for money.
- Improve commitments to business needs based on priorities.
- Decrease dependencies on IT and improve turnaround time.

Project Portfolio Management

- Prioritize projects.
- Resource planning.
- Application rationalization.

IT Governance

- Establish governance team and encourage best practices.
- Enforce data quality compliance.

People and Processes

- Document business processes for the seven disciplines.
- Cross-discipline processes not consistently followed.
- Focused training.

RESULTS OF ASSESSMENT

Business Challenges:

- Business processes not well documented and the mapping between the workflow unknown.
- General communication challenges considering the distributed work environment.
- Adequate governance not in place for business processes.
- Multiple systems need to be updated manually via rekey, leading to less productivity.
- Contract management done manually and requires extensive follow-up with suppliers.
- Available business applications cumbersome; most business applications siloed with multiple data entry points.
- Manual aggregation of data leads to bottleneck that requires unit and district managers' time; school districts' personnel's time spent reconciling point of service data into current system.
- Budgeting process for schools cumbersome, time-consuming.

IT Challenges

- Most systems, including finance and ERP (employee resource planning), in silos, not integrated with other mainstream systems.
- Lack of necessary control over existing system and its inefficiencies among users leads to need for a viable alternative.
- Need to implement industry standard processes defined for architecture and design.
- Possibility to automate integration/interfaces and help reduce manual dependencies.
- IT governance process and project management practices need to be defined and put in place.
- Need to identify architectural and process opportunities to maximize the existing IT investment.
- Need plan to scale up using the existing investment in applications and systems.

The Challenge:

To create a cohesive food management solution that assimilates the operations of enterprise resource planning, finance, and production on a single platform. The information also has to be presented in a manner to increase user engagement for all the stakeholders—from dieticians, nutritionists, food services directors, and chefs to warehouse managers, field operators, and line employees. All this had to ensure operational success, reduce the margin of errors, and comply with government rules and regulations as well as provide role-based access to the system that takes into account security and privacy laws.

The Solution:

A comprehensive, mobile-enabled, modular, and SaaS (software as a service) Cloud-based enterprise resource planning solution that automates the food service business. With modules for nutrition and front-office management, the system seamlessly connects the supply chain with the front and back offices. Its primary functions include recipes, product and vendor management, menu planning, nutritional analysis, allergen and ingredient tracking, inventory management, revenue management, procurement process, and production record generation.

IN SHORT:

AS IS. . . (the current situation)

Business. . .

- Ineffective communication.
- Business processes inefficient; lack of governance leads to inefficiencies.
- Contract management inadequate.
- Stock inventory inadequate and often leads to production halt.

Technology. . .

- Offline business reporting (multiple systems not talking to each other).
- Multiple rekey required; multiple applications do not sync data, making rekey mandatory.
- Data untrustworthy; not clean and lack of data definitions.

TO BE. . .(future resolutions)

Business. . .

- Implement unified communication system.
- Governance will define the business.

Technology. . .

- Implement custom solution to replace off-the-shelf system.
- Collapse business applications under one umbrella to enable entry once, multiple use.
- IT processes streamlined and standardized.
- Access unified data via the common interface.

RESULTING COST SAVINGS:

- Nearly $4 million over a five-year conversion plan with platform instead of licensing and servicing fees in previous system.
- Additional benefits:
  - Improved and more and better customer experience.
  - Improved and more and better employee experience.
  - Exponential growth.

PART II

BECOME THE DISRUPTOR

CHAPTER 5

Building Your Digital Road Map

Digital transformation isn't a sprint; it's a marathon journey.

Digital isn't new; we've all been on the journey for years. What is new, however, is the urgency to embrace the digital platform as a pathway to disrupt for business survival.

To lay out the road map for a company's transformation—the DOM playbook—first requires an assessment of where a company is today on its journey to digital maturity and the possibilities for the future. Taking another tack, the assessment is about identifying the pain points for your company, its people, and its customers whether related to culture, platform, or innovation.

Over time businesses accumulate "fat" in their organization—processes that are obsolete but still used—or even poor data that lacks consistency and does little more than clog the systems and experiences. For example, some companies still require a customer to submit a voided check to set up automatic payments instead of authenticating a user with their bank account or using approved payment platforms.

Those inefficiencies need to be cleaned up so that data/processes can flow smoothly for your people and your customers. Then it's possible to recognize what is required to help your company move forward on its digital journey, and determine step-by-step how to develop the framework to get there.

DIFFERENT JOURNEYS

One size does not fit all. A company's journey to digital transformation varies depending on where the company is located, its industry, and size.

Simplicities and Complexities

Companies in developed countries like the United States often must deal with entrenched legacy systems and operations and how to build them into any digital modernization. That compares with emerging economies in countries like South Africa, Brazil, China, and India that can build from scratch and in turn accelerate the digital journey.

Bigger companies have bigger systems, more layers, more people, and more departments and subdepartments that take longer to thoroughly assess, build out a road map, and incrementally implement change. Some industries are more complex with more layers and more rules and regulations too. Yet, all companies must deal with data, process, and experience.

A food service company, for example, must deal with myriad external public health and safety regulations as well as layers of internal controls, external logistics, lots of people, and more. That compares with perhaps a machine tool company that might manufacture a single relatively simple product or a software company with all digital assets.

Implementing a DOM at Whitsons or HHS—both food-related companies—has more layers and takes more time than the transformation for a much smaller and limited-in-scope print shop or coffee machine manufacturer.

Important Strategy

However, smaller companies absolutely should look to a well-thought-out digital operating model to compete and succeed in today's highly competitive marketplace. A digital operating model enhances a company's ability to individually deliver the best customer service with greater customization, fewer errors, and more consistency. Think dependability and trust in products, services, and experiences.

At the core of successful digital transformation is the purpose-driven strategy that begins with clearly knowing and understanding your customers and your customers' customers. Let's again look at the milk cooperative mentioned in previous chapters, and how its business platform's data, processes, and customer experiences—positive and negative—affected the dairy giant's choice to embrace the digital journey. As touched on earlier, the company was experiencing data inconsistencies that complicated its processes and compromised its customers' experiences. Internally there were mistakes in data that was collected and externally sent to customers. All that challenged the long-standing trust built up among the company, its customers, and their customers. The cooperative's suppliers are paid based on the weight and quantity of product delivered, so if the numbers are off, potentially members could earn less.

After a thorough assessment of the operations that identified the challenges and the issues internally and externally, the company implemented a DOM that all but eliminated errors, enhanced customer service and trust, and increased operating efficiencies. The company's and its customers' data are now consistently reliable, accurate, and secure. Its internal processes and customer experiences are more streamlined and efficient, too.

DATA QUALITY A DIFFERENTIATOR

As the milk cooperative recognized, the quality of a company's data matters. Whether that data relates to products, services, processes, experiences, or customers, it's a differentiator from the competition. The data itself as well as how it's managed or not helps determine the health of a business and its success or lack of success.

Just as we clean and service our vehicles, a business and its data require servicing and clean-up. For some companies, digital transformation begins with simply getting their house in order—cleaning up the data, analyzing it, knowing what's valuable and what's not, and delivering on the experience.

What's in a Name?

Without the right management, data cannot be advantageously monetized and that can lead to problems. That's because data definitions vary from system to system within companies and create inconsistencies.

Consider something as simple as how a company defines a client name and subsequently enters it into its various systems. Even more basic, does the company take the time to define how—manually or electronically—to record a client's name? Every company should, because without clear definitions for even the simplest data entries like a name, that data's value is limited.

Let's look at a university that has siloed operations—a typical situation for all different kinds and sizes of businesses. Academics are on one system; personnel another; student systems, another; buildings and maintenance, another; and finance on yet another. Even if the systems are compatible—which they often aren't across a business—the value of the data and the systems' capabilities depend on the quality of the data definitions.

At this university, the names of students, faculty, and providers are, based on practice—the data definition—input on one system as first name, last name. Another system stipulates that names are input as last name first, first name last. And still another system utilizes a process that lists names as first name, middle initial, last name.

All this sounds confusing and not just when we talk about it, or whether the data is entered manually or electronically. The data on each system may work well on that system, but when connected with another system—a platform ecosystem—the data for the users then becomes irrelevant. Even the most advanced business platform ecosystem can't differentiate all this data accurately. It's *garbage in, garbage out*. In fact, the university's data then becomes relatively useless—what we call inorganic and unhealthy. And it can't be optimized across the university or in any other way.

The solution isn't about laying blame. The situation isn't any one person's fault, either. As most any business grows, usually it keeps buying new products for siloed business objectives that in the long run create more complexities.

Healthy Approach—Data Unification

However, consider what happens when the university approaches its data management with integration in mind and makes sure all names are input in the same manner. The data definition, for example, calls for names to appear as last name first, followed by first name and middle initial. In a business platform, this is referred to as a common data model.

Suddenly, that data and the information that can be gleaned from it becomes valuable. It's accurate and possible to assess past, present, and future trends, directions, and potential needs. Interactions by consumers, educators, students, and personnel can be tracked across all departments in the university. As a result, the university gains an accurate and healthy picture of its needs and shortcomings and the data flows across the business end to end smoothly.

The health of *your* business hinges on the health of your data. Has your company made the effort to define its data and work to make sure that data remains healthy so that your business can thrive on its digital journey?

Can you track your data—even a single piece—end to end in the company? You should be able to successfully. If not, then why not? Very often companies rely on common data models—a series of definitions or explanations of various data, its relationship to entities in a business, its purpose, and so on. Utilizing a common data model helps maintain the integrity of the data and how it's used.

HOLISTIC APPROACH

To get an accurate picture of where a company is on its digital journey requires a holistic approach. After all, digital transformation affects the entire business and is about integrating all parts of the business.

Doctor's Analogy

When someone is sick, they often contact or visit a medical professional for diagnosis and treatment. That professional doesn't take one quick look at the patient and immediately announce what's wrong or immediately prescribe treatment. Rather they examine the patient, explore potential issues by asking questions, checking symptoms, and running tests. Then, with all the test results in hand, they offer a diagnosis and prescribe treatment.

The same kind of complexities are involved in assessing the digital health—or lack thereof—of a business. That's because the right digital solutions—as discussed in these chapters—aren't one dimensional. The prescription for good business health starts with an assessment and understanding of business processes as well as the entire business system end to end.

The best solutions also aren't prefaced with "throw out everything and start over." Instead, they usually involve figuring out how to marry existing systems with new ones to optimize operations and consumer and customer experiences. We've talked about companies like Crum & Forster, Whitsons, and others that have done this successfully.

Steps in Assessment

Some questions to consider in assessing your company's digital transformation status include:

- Where are we today—As Is?
- Where do we want to be tomorrow—To Be?
- What's our business and IT strategy—currently and moving forward?
- What's our road map or pathway to DOM?
- What is an achievable ROR (rate of return) versus the traditional ROI (return on investment)?
- What are our next moves?

Complexities and Simplicities

Returning to the human health analogy, consider how the human body functions. Various organs—including essentials like the brain, heart, lungs, kidneys, and liver—each have their own function and all work together, hopefully smoothly, to keep the blood flowing throughout the body and all the other processes working seamlessly.

A business similarly has essential organs or elements that work together to nurture it—finance, marketing, human resources, production, customer service, and so on. The lifeblood to a business is its data, which, when optimized, nurtures growth and development across all aspects of that business.

Like an organ in the human body, each element in a business has a purpose and provides its value to the business. Even a small business requires all parts in some form to work together to survive and thrive. If one part comes up short or is left out, the business weakens and eventually crumbles.

With a thorough assessment or prescription for good health, a company can put together the right platform—DOM—to seamlessly and consistently deliver its goods and/or services to customers and consumers. All elements of the business operations in turn will work together smoothly. The data will flow through the various business processes to deliver customer experiences. Think of healthy data flow as blood flowing through and nourishing a healthy human body. When the data flows properly, it generates revenues whether the business has $5 billion in revenues or $5 million. Then the business can achieve its purpose, scale, and grow exponentially.

Taking Stock

Here are a few more things to think about when considering a company's digital status. The answers to the following questions may not be readily available, but nonetheless think about them as you begin an assessment.

Where is the company in terms of the three essential elements for digital transformation: culture, architecture or platform, and innovation? Are all three elements present in the business? If so, great, you're on your way. If not, what's missing and why? What needs to happen to facilitate change?

What about business processes? Likely some may be manual, others automated, some connected, and some not. Without streamlined processes, experiences are not optimized. There can be data inconsistencies and inaccuracies, too, that can be a threat to customer trust. In making your assessments, pay attention to what works and what doesn't, and the strengths and weaknesses of each aspect of the business.

Other areas of a business and its operations that need to be examined include:

- Architecture: process, development, communication, and governance.
- Business linkage.
- Data definitions.
- Information technology in general.
- IT investment and acquisition strategy.
- Operating unit participation.
- Senior management involvement.

Business Flow

To help identify data inconsistencies and inaccuracies in a business, draw an end-to-end business flow diagram that includes:

- Where your business product or service starts.
- Where it ends.
- What all the department touchpoints are.
- How many systems and functions are running smoothly.
- How many need improvements.
- How many need a change.

As Is and To Be

The best assessment of where a company stands on its digital journey does not just address today, but also looks ahead to tomorrow—*As Is* and *To Be*. To Be represents what once was only a dream for the future and now is possible with a digital operating model in place. And those assessments must relate to the business side of a company and on the technology side.

Done right, the assessment of a business then becomes the beginning of a digital road map for what can be accomplished in the future. It's the guide to building a shopping mall–like business platform that shows where you are and where you can go tomorrow.

All Things Possible

A San Francisco–based healthcare company struggled with long patient admission times and the lack of availability of personalized patient health information. The company's thorough assessment singled out problem areas that included time-consuming and tedious traditional paper-based processes and poor patient data security. Because of its industry—healthcare—any digital solutions also had to be compliant with the Health Insurance Portability and Accountability Act (HIPAA) that ensures patient data confidentiality.

The company's DOM solution included creation of digital patient cards instead of paper ones and a web-based user interface as well as safe and secure Cloud storage for patient information—all HIPAA-compliant.

With the DOM in place, patient data and records now are more secure. Information is easily accessible. Admission times have been slashed by 65%. Efficiency of healthcare services delivery is up more than 70% and business revenues are up 43%.

DOM IN MOTION

As we examine the levels to digital maturity, again remember that a digital operating model revolves around three elements: culture, platform, and innovation. When all three elements work together to help mature the company's data, processes, and experiences, that's a DOM in motion. As the velocity of that DOM increases, so does the speed of a company's growth toward digital maturity.

Before we look closer at important actions associated with the five levels, let's look at some things to consider when it comes to how a business handles its processes. With the shopping mall analogy in mind, remember that businesses typically break down processes into two categories: vertical and horizontal. The vertical parts of a business include the company's core revenue-generating and growth functions like sales and marketing, line production, product development, and so on. The horizontal functions include support systems like employee management—HR, administrative services, cost optimization, and employee experience.

Now let's look briefly at some concerns at the various stages or levels a company goes through on the journey to digital maturity. Digital maturity happens when a company moves from simple digitization—converting existing data and processes to digital format—to digitalization. The latter is about embracing the potential digital has to offer.

Level 1: Digital Infancy

This is the starting point—initial basic awareness that digital exists and is supposed to make life easier. This could be a new business with a new idea or a legacy business with little or no automation. These companies remain small and likely will be disrupted. Their digital assets primarily are printed reports.

Some dos and don'ts for this level include:

- Do understand that digital is more than simply technology.
- Do let go of old manual processes and be open to change.
- Don't automatically assume digital is beyond reach physically, financially, or in terms of technology awareness and complexities.
- Do explore ways to grow your business and how digital can help.
- Don't be afraid to think about ways to streamline your operations, improve accuracy, and bolster customer service and connections.

Level 2: Early Experiments

Many companies today are at this digital junction, whether out of personal choice or by default thanks to the 2020–2021 work-from-home mandate due to COVID-19 lockdowns. Companies at this level realize they are losing business and employees to competitors and now are willing to change.

Some dos and don'ts for this level include the above in Level 1 plus:

- Do take time for a thorough digital assessment of not only your technology, but your business processes, culture, and people skills, too.
- Do encourage your people to imagine the possibilities that a DOM can mean for the business. The impossible is possible with digital.
- Don't think in terms of siloed, top-down processes.
- Do empower your people to take the initiative, to innovate, and to make decisions.

Level 3: Digitally Credible

Companies at this level are moving forward slowly on their digital strategy. They are exploring existing investments and looking at opportunities to exploit what they have. They realize that to digitalize their core business systems they must define vertical and horizontal systems.

Some dos and don'ts for this level include the above in Levels 1 and 2 plus:

- Don't give up or become complacent with people who are holdouts to change and unwilling to let go of the status quo.
- Do encourage innovation at all levels.
- Do take the time to assess what's working and what's not, and let go of what's not.
- Don't settle for the status quo or ordinary growth projections. Exponential growth is fast-becoming table stakes with digital.

Level 4: Digitally Mature

These companies have organized their businesses as platforms and truly can be called digitalized. They function like a mall, with shared services where applicable and with clarity of end-to-end business processes. Customer/employee interactions happen through digital channels.

Some dos and don'ts for this level include the above in Levels 1, 2, and 3 plus:

- Do encourage out-of-the-box innovative thinking. Remember, the impossible is possible with a DOM. The future of your business is at stake.

- Do have an "innovation lab" to quickly and on a small scale test new ideas, processes, and products.
- Do work to allow those holdouts to change or work themselves out of your company.
- Do seamlessly mesh business and technology into one homogeneous culture.
- Do hire and encourage your people to have adaptability at all levels of the business.
- Don't become complacent.

Level 5: The Market Leaders

Companies at this level have reached continuous digital maturity. These are the disruptors and market leaders that compete with themselves. Innovation is pivotal as is seeking ways to competitively differentiate themselves and their products or services with the help of this level of digital whether it relates to data, process, or experience.

These companies represent a DOM in motion: a business platform where data, process, and experience move at a high velocity. Their digital assets include the ability to add new systems to a platform easily and to unplug digital assets that have become obsolete. These companies are leaders in data maturity with data science and artificial intelligence and they have the ability to monetize their data.

To remain on top and avoid backsliding, some dos and don'ts at this level include:

- Do consistently keep building and discovering new ways to service your market.
- Do maintain a high-performing culture.
- Do retain high-performing talents.
- Don't become complacent.
- Don't lose sight of the goal to deliver better experiences to customers via seamless processes, especially when adding new components and capabilities to your platform.
- Don't allow your platform ecosystem to revert back to a hodgepodge of systems.

YOUR DIGITAL QUIZ

No matter the company, industry, or where on the digital transformation journey a company is today, absolutely don't automatically assume that digital is beyond reach. A legacy company with lots of siloed operations or a small company with mostly manual operations can be ready for digital transformation.

A thorough digital assessment most likely will yield surprising results about a company and the digital journey.

The Questions

The following are some more questions to consider. Think about each one and how it might relate to your various business operations as well as your people and customers. There are no right or wrong answers to the questions, only the goal of a holistic look at the present digital state of a business and what's possible for the future.

1. **Does the company have a clear definition and stated objective for its journey to digital maturity and beyond? What does the company hope to gain, both internally and externally?** The answers to these questions revolve around a common vision for growth and aligning executives/leaders with frontline workers who deliver the experiences. Continuously changing consumer and customer behaviors also plays a role; therefore, rigidity no longer works. A business platform offers the necessary fluidity and adaptability.

2. **Is the company looking for a quick implementation of key digital initiatives or for a long-term strategy?** Keep in mind that quick fixes aren't a solution or valid approach to the disrupt-or-be-disrupted mantra, especially in light of today's intense competition. Again, think of your business in the context of a shopping mall. That mall requires effective planning and isn't built overnight. The space must be designed; the building constructed; space leased to retailers and service providers; stores designed; and finally service providers and staff employed to manage operations.

   Similarly, a business platform must be designed using a Cloud or hybrid model; plans must take into consideration how consumers and customers will effectively use the tools, and then their development/ procurement prioritized. Irrespective of whether a tool is off-the-shelf or custom built, it must fit into the platform ecosystem in the right order.

With the right platform in place, replacing or upgrading one system is as easy as replacing a tenant in the mall.

3. **Does the company already utilize a Cloud platform or SaaS (software as a service) anywhere in its systems and execution? For example, does the company pay a monthly or annual fee for the use of any software or processes? In other words, do its people access the Cloud—the internet—for any process or service?** Even an operating system like Microsoft 365 utilizes a Cloud platform and counts as beginning steps on the digital journey. A robust business platform includes all of the above—Cloud, on-premise apps, SaaS, bespoke apps (tailored to a specific company's needs), and combinations of any of these apps.

4. **Does the organization have an agile or fluid culture, especially in delivering technology solutions? Can the company shift direction quickly as markets and needs dictate? Think about how the company reacted to the work-from-home edict as part of the pandemic lockdown. Was it able to relatively smoothly get its operations and distant people connected? Did the company utilize a communications and collaboration platform?** When a company matures in its business platform, it becomes fluid and adaptable to change. Hence, during the pandemic, companies that matured with their platform could accelerate faster than other companies that had to learn and train their people along the way. Keep in mind that people learn faster when they don't have a choice.

5. **Does the company have a formal DevOps group, operation, or plan?** That's tech jargon for combining IT and software development to streamline operations. Automation of software development is an example. Automation of a business or software building process is a milestone to measure a company's level of platform maturity. Work that is repetitive and tedious should be a candidate for automation.

6. **Does the company have comprehensive enterprise architecture in place?** Just as city planning encompasses all aspects of city operations and its growth and development, enterprise architecture addresses all aspects of operations of a business now and into the future. Every building or civil infrastructure must have solid architecture and a foundation. Similarly, a digital platform will not exist without enterprise architecture. When people build an app for one objective, the architecture is solo technical architecture. But when all aspects of the business are thought through, the same architecture emerges as enterprise architecture and evolves as a business platform.

7. **How would you describe the company's IT department: in-house, outsourced, hybrid, or something else? What happens when there's a problem with technology? Who solves it and how?** It can be lean management, in-house, or outsourced. What matters is that as long as the company works with fewer people, has full transparency, and agility, it can be digitally savvy. Technology always has problems so planning for a robust app management by a vendor or in-house team is necessary. (Of note: design a service-level agreement that manages applications with three levels of support mechanisms based on time involved and complexities.)

8. **Are there systems in place to manage processes? If so, are they connected? If not, what is and isn't connected?** A good system manages business processes to deliver either customer or employee experiences. Every business has its own workflows and rules. Good software can map them end to end. Usually employee-facing apps are separate from customer-facing ones as part of the business platform.

9. **Has the company successfully rolled out solutions like chatbots (automated customer service options), machine learning (automated data analysis), or other artificial intelligence solutions?** These are all must-have technologies for the future and for a business to remain relevant. As today's customers become more accustomed to automated methods to interact with companies, tools like voice, chatbots, and AI are gaining popularity.

10. **Does the company leverage the API economy effectively? Remember, API is computer jargon for application programming interface, the ability of different applications and devices to talk to each other.** Not every platform will have all the business features that allow collaboration. For example, a voice-activated speaker can connect with multiple screens, but only if those screens are compatible. It's impossible to get a solution from just one box when a company relies on the marketplace to buy or build new solutions. And, it's increasingly more complex to connect all of them seamlessly (through API) so that they act as one system.

Developing a Clear Picture

Addressing these questions should paint a clearer, more realistic picture of the present and future potential for a company on its digital development pathway. Most likely, the results show the company is farther along on the journey than initially thought or expected. After all, it's easy to overlook some of the simplest tasks and operations that already rely on the Cloud, platforms, and/or software for success.

On closer inspection, what likely becomes clearer, too, are the shortcomings—the extent of disparate and disconnected functions and operations—in a business. Even companies that think they're on the road to digital transformation still may have siloed systems as opposed to streamlined platform operations; a mix of manual and tedious tasks with some digital operations operating independently; redundancies in tasks as well as data collection; few, if any, standardized data definitions; and lack of IT expertise. Lack of a concrete data strategy, missing a future development plan (a digital road map), as well as modern and monetized data systems and infrastructure are also common challenges.

Whitsons and Quest are great examples of companies that, after thoroughly assessing their digital health, realized they needed to take steps necessary to develop the right DOM for theirs needs and enhance their products, services, and growth in the process.

Remember Global Furniture Group? When Ari Asher came in to head up operations in its U.S. division, initially he considered recommending the replacement of the company's ERP system. But then on closer assessment, he realized the company first needed to get its processes right before it could leverage technology to its benefit.

Your Digital Scorecard

A company's level of digital maturity revolves around data, process, and experience. To determine where your business stands, rate each of the following aspects of your business on a scale of 1 to 5 with 5 the highest level of maturity—market leader.

Client and Employee Experience:

- Client communication and feedback.
- Client onboarding.
- Client interface and real-time experience.
- Consistency of experience.
- Growth network.

- Employees' systems: availability of the right information at the right time.
- Employee collaboration.
- Effective business process and role-based access.

Business Process:

- Strategy–leadership alignment, governance, and compliance.
- Tools that are easy to scale.
- Availability and access of key performance indicators and dashboard analytics.
- Operational efficiency and accuracy.
- Adaptability to change processes easily.
- Ability to automate the new process.

Data:

- Accuracy.
- Consistency.
- Stored in a format with the ability to easily extract data.
- Data structure in a format that can provide intelligence.
- Reasonable cost to manage.
- Trust and privacy assured.
- Ability to automate the data.

DIGITAL RESILIENCY

Whatever the details of the digital journey ahead for a company, expect it to be a long one—the marathon mentioned earlier. However, the length or the nature of the journey shouldn't discourage anyone from taking the journey. To succeed at anything requires ongoing commitment. That commitment is not because the journey necessarily is so difficult, but because its results are so far-reaching and transformative across all aspects of a company and its people.

The recipe for digital success calls for resiliency and determination by the company, its leadership, and its people to get the job done. That means ongoing discussion about the changes and future possibilities while consistently working hard to stay the course with the end goals in mind.

When It Works. . .

In these pages, you've already learned how the DOM journey changed the future for so many different companies. Yet each began with an assessment that led to a road map to the pathway to change and growth.

Mastercard has been an innovator in its space for years. The company has been traditionally a card payments scheme and network where change meant slight technology alterations and upgrades; today it is about disruption and exponential growth. In the context of current world culture, that's expanding beyond card and chips to QR codes, contactless electronic payments, money transfers, and instantaneous transactions.

Mastercard assessed As Is and To Be, framed its vision, laid out a road map, and began to work toward that vision with innovative new ideas internally and through acquisition. The company acquired London-based Vocalink Holdings Ltd., which operates key account-to-account payments technology platforms in the United Kingdom and elsewhere. (More on that later.)

Mastercard's leaders understand, too, the importance of tackling challenges to best augment the experience of its people, customers, and customer's customers. In one of its more recent transformations the corporation wanted to create a richer customer experience by introducing an application that makes paying bills through online and mobile banking seamless, fast, error-free, and easy for the banks, billers, and consumers.

Leveraging the value of multiple platforms, the company was able to relatively simply bolster its offerings, including:

- Core functionality: allows billers to submit an electronic payment request via the consumer banking app (with all payment/account information included).
- Allow users to view all bills, choose when and how to pay, and communicate directly with the biller (the biller sets the reminders, not the payer).
- Billers get better transparency of when payment will be received. Billers may receive funds instantly, if the consumer chooses to pay that way, with reduced risk of nonsufficient funds or chargebacks.
- Billers can improve internal operating efficiencies (e.g. supports automatic reconciliation of payments with customer accounts) plus ability to communicate directly re: enquiries/disputes improves customer experience and satisfaction.

. . .When It Doesn't

Remember the university in Leicester, England, and its initial failed attempt to embrace the digital operating model a number of years ago? And, what about the Midwestern food services management company that fell short with digital transformation?

In both cases, there was plenty of talk about the possibilities of digital, but not the commitment across the board to get it done Hence, their digital journeys came up short.

BUILDING YOUR ROAD MAP

Now it's your turn to move forward on the digital journey. Think about your company: what is now and what could be tomorrow.

Before beginning the actual company-wide assessment, try learning more about and reviewing the process. Again, every company's journey is different. And not everyone will enthusiastically embrace digital at first.

To facilitate that change at your company, think about the business's objectives. Not everyone wants to be a Crum & Forster, an Amazon, or a McDonald's. But companies of all shapes and sizes like the idea of being in existence tomorrow and turning a profit in the process.

PATHWAYS TO GROWTH: A ROUNDUP

- To get an accurate assessment of where a company is on its digital journey requires a holistic approach much like a doctor examines a patient first before making a diagnosis.

- An assessment is about knowing and understanding your business end to end. That includes processes, data, and experience internally (horizontally) and externally (with your customers).

- The best assessment of where a company stands on its digital journey includes a picture of today—As Is—as well as tomorrow—To Be. Assessments must relate to the business as well as technology sides of a company.

- Done right, the assessment of a business then becomes the beginning of a digital road map to what can be accomplished in the future. It's the guide to building a shopping mall–like business platform that shows where you are and where you can go tomorrow.

- A business assessment uncovers shortcomings like the extent of disparate and disconnected functions and operations; siloed systems as opposed to streamlined platform operations; a mix of manual and tedious tasks with some digital operations operating independently; redundancies in tasks as well as data collection; few, if any, standardized data definitions; and lack of IT expertise.
- Lack of a concrete data strategy, missing a future development plan (a digital road map), as well as modern and monetized data systems and infrastructure are also common challenges businesses face.

CHAPTER 6

Unleashing the Power of Your Business Platform

In a digital world every voice matters. Listen.

After a thorough and honest assessment of As Is and To Be, a company should know where it is on the DOM journey today, its strengths and shortcomings in terms of the three elements—culture, platform, and innovation—and have a vision for the future.

Now it's time to take the next step, to lay out the road map to fix the pain points, and aim for the dreams of the future. Let's look at how to put together the right digital operating model to meet your company's needs. Keep in mind that DOM helps get your house in order and comes with ease of scalability, applicable privacy, and compliance rules and regulations in place.

With a DOM, as markets and marketplaces change, quick pivots are the norm. Compliance changes are no problem; neither are add-ons and changes. Business platforms have the ability for easy plug and play. This is integration at its best. That doesn't mean that transformation to digital maturity among the various levels is always smooth. But when all the elements are in place and a business is organized on a platform—the shopping mall analogy—experiences are easier and more seamless for employees and customers.

MEASURING YOUR PROGRESS: EXPLORE/ EXPLOIT/DISRUPT

Scaling up is a challenge for almost every business whether on the journey to digital maturity or not. Those that have embraced digital maturity, though, have the advantage of a road map to the future. With that road map—the assessment of As Is and To Be in hand—companies already know where they are today, where they are going, and what it will take to get there.

As discussed in previous chapters, most businesses have untapped potential whether related to people, digital or manual assets, products, partners or services, and more. The first step toward digital maturity is about exploring the full potential of what you have, and then leveraging those assets in the best ways possible.

Once a company embraces the DOM, it becomes a matter of explore, exploit, and then disrupt with the power of digital.

Some questions to consider on that journey include:

- Is company growth stagnant or linear? Why hasn't exponential growth happened yet? What's missing? Are your processes tailored to your digital platform or are your people trying to use outdated processes with new technology—the square peg in the round hole?
- How many users are on the platform? Are your teams adopting the new technology? If not, why not?
- How many lives have been improved either internally with your teams or externally with your customers with the help of a business platform? If not many, then it's time to figure out why not. What are the bottlenecks?

THE INDIAFIRST LIFE JOURNEY

Today IndiaFirst Life Insurance Company Limited is promoted by two of India's largest public-sector banks—Bank of Baroda and Union Bank of India, which hold 65% and 9% stakes in the company, respectively. Carmel Point Investments India Private Limited incorporated by Carmel Point Investment Ltd., a body corporate incorporated under the laws of Mauritius and owned by private equity funds managed by Warburg Pincus LLC, New York, also holds a 26% stake in IndiaFirst Life.

Vishakha R M, its CEO and Managing Director, has ensured that the culture of a "happy, passionate, and connected" workplace continues.

The company retains its four-time certification as a Great Place to Work®, too, and also has been featured as one of India's Best Workplaces for Women 2021.

Since inception, the organization had a disruptive vision for India's life insurance industry. The company's leaders were ready and willing to disrupt the industry; platform technology was on the table, and the innovation was there.

CEO Vision

The year was 2012 and IndiaFirst Life's then managing director and CEO wanted to automate the insurance business end to end with a digital operating model. The vision was to sell life insurance policies and handle claims and client services through one platform ecosystem.

Since the company was new, it had no legacy systems and related issues to manage. That gave it the advantage of being able to more quickly build a new business platform to disrupt the market. However, what happened with IndiaFirst Life shows how a business's culture and an audacious vision set by a CEO may not be enough to penetrate all ranks within an organization and stall the digital journey and growth as a result.

IndiaFirst Life built a next-generation underwriting and claims management system and bought ready-made systems to manage its HR, sales, and administrative processes. That helped accelerate the DOM model. But IndiaFirst Life remained stalled at Level 2/early experimenters in its evolution to digital maturity.

Question of Processes

The company's pivotal moment came in 2015 with its new leader, Vishakha R M. The company already had the digital road map and business platform in place and had been focused on exploring and exploiting its new investment. Vishakha focused on digitizing and automating the business processes. She put together a change management group focused on effectively disseminating the digital mindset across organizational levels to help fulfil the potential of the existing business platform. The group digitized its underwriting and claims management process and integrated it with the policy administration system and rules engine to enable straight through processing of underwriting rules. That significantly improved the customer experience. For example, IndiaFirst Life replaced its customer consent process based on wet signatures with a simple one-time password-based acknowledgment, taking away the dependency of meeting the customer in person for their consent on an application form.

Holistic Approach

To be successful, the quest for digital maturity requires an all-encompassing approach. A company—in this instance, IndiaFirst Life—can't fit old and inadequate processes into new surroundings. Rather, the new surroundings are complemented by the organized business platform that holds data, processes, and experiences in the right place in the business ecosystem.

As with IndiaFirst Life, when a company merges a business platform and mindset, it progresses on its journey to digital maturity. IndiaFirst Life has advanced to Level 3/digitally credible.

THE COMMONALITIES

The good news is that no matter the size of a company or its industry, the framework for a digital operating model is the same. It's back to the presence of the three elements:

- Culture
- Business platform
- Innovation

A business platform is critical when a company's culture is ready to support building and maturing it. Once the components of the business platform—data, process, and experience—are well understood and organized, it's easier for frontline workers to demand the change, and the back-end office can quickly pivot to meet market demands. This method works irrespective of the industry or company size.

Let's look closer first at aligning the elements, and then later some tips on the five levels of digital maturity.

CULTURE/MINDSET

We've established that people come first. For successful change to work, a company's culture—its people—must have a transformative mindset and be ready for change.

What does your digital assessment say about your people and change? Are they ready and on board across all levels? What about your CEO and managers? Or are they settled in their ways and figure it's "working" so why change? If it's the latter, then no matter the size of a company, transformation can't happen without first a culture shift.

Even if customers complain about long time frames to get things done and data inaccuracies, or your people protest tedious tasks, that doesn't mean change is always welcome. All the innovation alone isn't enough to fuel movement to the next level of DOM without help.

Change Management Works

That's where the right change management strategy comes in. After India-First Life's Vishakha R M took over as CEO, she maintained the focus of her predecessor for a time, exploring and exploiting the digital investments.

But eventually it was time to refocus, to do what was necessary to take the next step into a high-growth phase, says Vishakha. "It was about saying, 'Okay, we created what we have for five years. Now how do we improve those processes? How do we eliminate what is redundant because technology has changed so much?'"

Change management ensued. The company assessed what worked well and what didn't. Teams worked to reinforce broad acceptance of more streamlined and efficient processes, and the company resumed its forward momentum on the digital transformation journey.

Steps to Take

When it comes to your company, hopefully your thorough digital assessment identified those people in the company with a transformative mindset—who is and isn't ready for change? This isn't a purge; it's about getting everyone together to move forward to make lives and jobs easier and for company growth.

Where in the company are those people open to change physically located? Are they assigned to the main office, working remotely, or at a branch office? What are their departments and their jobs?

Change-makers should be dispersed throughout the company because peer pressure can be a positive force. Oftentimes shifting change-positive individuals into other positions and places where there is change hesitancy can help sway minds.

There are all types of books, articles, courses, and experts with advice on change management techniques and how to make it happen. In these pages you've read about some of the moves that companies have made to help change culture mindsets.

Whitsons, for example, made sure its leaders' future visions for the company were aligned. IndiaFirst Life dispersed change management teams throughout the company. No matter how the change management occurs in your company, the important thing is that it happens.

The Holdouts

Also, pay attention to who isn't willing to accept change. Can these individual holdouts be swayed? If so, leaders need to figure out what it will take to change these people's minds. The good news is that often those who are averse to change simply are afraid of the new and different and/or figure changes will jeopardize their jobs. Education and training that includes understanding someone's job isn't at risk can be enough to make the difference.

If someone still refuses to change, leaders must change the roles of Mr./Ms. Negative or help them realize they are in the wrong place. A company today cannot afford to explore all possibilities without the DOM and survive. And without buy-in by your people—especially at high management levels—exponential growth can falter.

Remember, at Levels 1 and 2 of the DOM companies are in the explore phase. By Levels 3 and 4, a company advances to explore and exploit because their business platforms have matured and they can exploit their data effectively. At Levels 4 and 5, a company explores, exploits, and disrupts because its culture and business platform are well-aligned; innovation is working and the business has recipes for disruption.

Tips to Encourage Change

As mentioned earlier, small incremental changes can often be easier to implement and a segue to larger ones down the road.

The right approach to hiring can encourage change, too. When positions open, look for technology-savvy people who like innovation and welcome change. Younger generations expect and accept the latest in technology. But that doesn't mean other generations don't have lots to offer and can't embrace the same changes and bells and whistles. After all, those older people *invented* the internet and digital. Companies have to be discerning and hire the right people for the right job, the company, and the road map ahead.

C&F's Gary McGeddy suggests you can create a culture that embraces change by pursuing the root of what causes human beings to not change, what he refers to as their negative inner dialog. That's kind of touchy-feely, he says, but when you invest in your people it creates a culture of extreme excellence and then you can accomplish whatever.

"The reason we grow at a steeper, consistent rate is because of all this investment we make in life and career coaching," says McGeddy. "We spend a tremendous amount of time and money in coaching our people. . .and getting them to recognize weaknesses and strengths in their personal and business lives and converting that into productivity in the workplace."

BUSINESS PLATFORM

Next, let's examine your business's platform. That's those legacy processes and architecture already in place that create a business's ecosystem. It could be homegrown, vendor provided, rented, or some other combination. Whatever the situation, consider that sometimes we buy a system for a specific purpose and no matter how badly we want to keep that system in the business as a showpiece, in the long run it's irrelevant.

A crucial aspect of the road map to becoming a more efficient and effective business involves figuring out the best way to utilize existing systems and assets—including people—and how to monetize them now and into the future.

It's back to exploring what works, what doesn't, what can be different and better, exploiting what you have, and then disrupting for exponential growth.

Think About It

With your existing processes and systems, consider a few of the following questions:

- **What works and what doesn't?** Be honest in the assessment.
- **What works but could work better?** Think in terms of customer as well as user experience.
- **How many touchpoints are there with customers and with employees?** Digital can help positively minimize those.

- **What areas/systems/architecture generate the most problems?** Those could be bottlenecks that slow things, or areas with the most customer or user complaints.
- **What architecture generates the fewest problems?** Even if it's an occasional problem, think about how the system or outcome could be improved.
- **What, if anything, is smooth sailing?** Simply because a process or procedure isn't new doesn't make it obsolete. It's essential to recognize what works well already.
- **If your system works "fine," is it truly leveraging the markets?** Are you exploiting your opportunities? What's missing?
- **Is your architecture/system equipped to handle the future?** Is it agile enough to change directions quickly with market demands and changes? If not, what's missing? What's holding you, your people, and your company back?

Be Selective

Remember the big U.S. newspaper mentioned in Chapter 3? The company already had embraced a DOM across some departments but hadn't yet embraced the power of a DOM in its advertising realm. The digitally savvy company didn't suddenly jettison everything in favor of starting over with the latest and greatest across the board.

Instead, the newspaper figured out its shortcomings and tossed only its outdated, inefficient, and cumbersome processes in favor of an internet-based business platform compatible with its other platforms. If something works well, keep it; if it doesn't, look to positive change.

Build versus Buy versus Rent

Build, buy, or rent has been a bottom-line conundrum for businesses big and small since the dawn of the digital age. Should a company build what it needs, buy off-the-shelf equipment and software, or rent the use of the process, software, or business platforms?

Companies of all sizes used to have to make huge cash outlays to buy the physical software—often not an exact fit for their needs—or build their own unique systems for their needs. Now the use of much of what's needed—or at the very least, the basics—is available online as a paid or sometimes even free or low-cost download or service.

New normal. This new normal today offers lots of opportunities to rent an app—SaaS (software as a service), for example, test the product or process, and if it doesn't work in your business, find something else. Businesses today must use these Cloud-based technologies to exploit their existing systems and processes.

Also as discussed, digital has leveled the playing field and slashed prices. With something as common as an operating system, a company used to have to pay tens of thousands to hundreds of thousands and even millions of dollars to obtain the physical software to plug into its systems. Worse, as soon as the purchase was made, the software already was outdated and required patches to be delivered or downloaded and installed. And every change or upgrade required additional costs, additional time and efforts with installation, and the inevitable cumbersome and complex glitches like lost data and IT compatibility issues.

But, thanks to today's platforms, it's a different story. With Cloud software, a company simply pays a monthly or annual fee for a set number of usage licenses, downloads the data, and it's automatically updated regularly. For CRM, for example, most companies tap into mature business platforms via SaaS. Or, in food service, companies look to BPaaS (business platforms as a service) offerings like next-generation food services management platforms.

When Whitsons initially began the digital journey, many of its systems were siloed, some off-the-shelf and some self-built. But there were difficulties. None of the systems were perfect, but all filled a need. Each was brought in at a time when Whitsons didn't know what it really needed, says CEO Paul Whitcomb. Adding to the bottlenecks, the off-the-shelf systems weren't necessarily targeted specifically to food service.

Leveraging investments. When the company decided to embrace the DOM model, Whitsons already had great finance and Salesforce software that worked well. So, the company was able to leverage that existing investment by modernizing it and combining it with a new vertical system to streamline its operations. It's the shopping mall: when a company's vertical systems and horizontal ones operate smoothly together on one platform ecosystem.

Then, as Whitsons found out so successfully, the platform effect happens. Once people see what can be accomplished with the platform, use of the new systems snowballs and growth is exponential.

Role of Integration in Business Platform

Again, think of your business like a shopping mall, as in Figure 6.1. In the mall, there are pathways that allow people to move between floors and reach

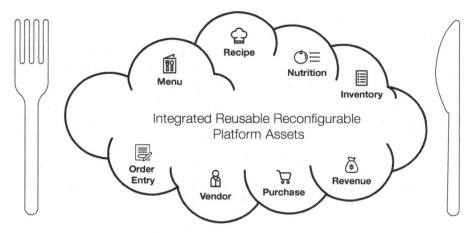

FIGURE 6.1   Food business platform.

relevant stores. Similarly in the tech world, there are pathways to creating a platform ecosystem. That could include API, bus architecture, integration layer, and middleware—all ways to connect multiple platforms and business components.

Without pathways, malls can't function. It's the same with these pathways that connect the various parts of a business platform. When we connect systems, we can exploit the platform, bring the right data at the right time, and rapidly solve problems.

DOM IN MOTION: WHERE TO BEGIN

So many available options, combined with the fact that every company's pathway to DOM is unique, can be scary, especially if someone isn't a technology wizard or sold on digital. But by taking the right steps one at a time, the challenges on the journey to digital maturity can be manageable.

Leaders and decision-makers should approach digital maturity with the idea that now the company, its people, and customers have the freedom to choose what they want, when they want it, and how they want it delivered. The choices aren't overwhelming; they offer opportunity. You can have it all easily and simply delivered.

"I didn't know yesterday what I know today," Al Hilal Life's Said Hathout says of the digital journey. "The journey itself was a learning."

With that approach, the sky can be the limit. A company can learn to exploit what it has and move forward to disrupt. New ideas and new processes then can evolve. Instead of one problem with one solution, the business platform offers multiple outcomes. Once a platform is in place, too, pivots and changes can be fast and efficient.

The journey will face roadblocks. With Whitsons, for example, CEO Paul Whitcomb says that in the beginning, his teams didn't really know what they wanted or the extent of a business platform's potential. "Even in some ways, 10 years later we still haven't achieved all the possibilities."

"We didn't know the extent of what technology could do," says Whitcomb.

That's yet more reason to think in terms of operating your business on a platform with tremendous potential for growth as well as the capability to handle the challenges ahead.

Back to the Assessment

Again, to lay the groundwork and chart the right road map, take the time for a thorough and holistic digital assessment to identify the weaknesses in your platform/architecture. Seek and listen to input from your people, your customers, your customer's customers, and even your competitors.

What is your biggest business challenge currently? What are the pain points? How does the competition handle a similar process, procedure, or challenge? What works and what doesn't? What does your decision-making process look like? For example, who are the key decision-makers and stakeholders, and what are the processes involved?

And what about demands for the future or potential changes in future markets and processes? Think ahead, think big, and think out of the box. What's the impossible dream? It can be possible with a digital operating model. With the answers to all these questions in mind, you can then make the targeted moves necessary to improve outcomes internally and externally.

Need versus Want

When it comes to technology, people and companies often don't know what they truly need versus what they want. Again, technology for technology's sake doesn't always solve the explicit problem.

Simply because something is the latest and greatest app, SaaS or BPaaS, or highly touted as the end-all and be-all in its space, doesn't mean it's the foolproof solution for everyone. That's been an issue for decades and will remain that way. DOM in motion, though, can provide the discipline to stay the course and not be swayed by the latest and greatest.

There also can be a big disconnect within departments of what they want versus what they need, says Rudy Sayegh, Founder and CEO of Global Gate Capital, an investment firm with offices in Geneva, London, New York, and Dubai that specializes in real estate, private equity, and wealth management. There are also times when the team doesn't know what they want, so they don't know the possibilities that existing systems can offer.

In other words, people may already have the tools and technology in front of them and don't know how to use them effectively. Sayegh suggests it's important for a company to prioritize. Assess what the business needs first and what comes next can be integrated on the road map to digital maturity. That's what his company did quite successfully.

It all goes back to the assessment of the shortcomings and weaknesses in As Is systems as well as looking forward to how a potential business platform can solve and serve needs of the future—To Be.

Then armed with that knowledge, it's much easier to identify the real needs, the necessary common assets—the mall concept again—and the best architecture to overcome the challenges.

INNOVATION

Implementing the third element of the DOM—innovation—is a bit trickier. That's because thinking about how to make the impossible possible is a tall order. Even though technology and science are involved, so are imagination and creativity, neither of which can be legislated or ordered on demand.

The Courage to Jump

Companies, accidently and purposely, often stymie innovation. It's not always a money issue either. It's because no one wants to be the first to jump forward with the new and different solution to challenges. The status quo will do.

Funny thing about that approach, though. Companies that hang back, that are afraid of innovation, usually are the first to want the new innovations when someone else takes the lead. But when a company considers failure as an experiment and success as a confidence builder, it has the ingredients to embrace innovation.

New ideas scare people, says Steve Butcher, formerly with the Higher Education Funding Council for England and involved with the university in Leicester, England, and its failed transformation discussed in Chapter 3. "As an IT manager told me 30 years ago, computer problems are people problems," he says.

From the Top

That's another reason companies must figure out how to encourage innovation. We talked about innovation labs as one way to foster new ideas and theories and then quickly test them to determine what works.

Encouraging innovation from the top—a key element of the digital operating model—also is essential. Executives need to foster an environment that welcomes and embraces new thoughts, ideas, processes, and approaches. The siloed top-down thinking of the past has no place in the DOM world.

As Crum & Forster's Marc Adee suggests, ideas need to bubble up and executives and leaders need to listen. By decentralizing his company's operations and empowering his people, Adee has created a more distributed approach to innovation. As a CEO, he's approachable and transparent.

"A lot of companies tried innovation labs—where a specific team was designated to come up with ideas. We went in the opposite direction," says Adee. "There is a lot more leverage when everyone is thinking about how we can improve—especially the people closer to the customer. Anyone can send me a note or an idea—and they do."

The Right Environment

Paul Hopkins, the innovative IT expert also involved with the Leicester university, says that when it comes to innovation, directors—chief executives—do not direct. Instead they need to create an environment that allows their people to excel. That means embracing and protecting innovation and disruptive thinking.

As David Granson of Goldman Sachs suggests when it comes to hiring the next generation of workers, "I'm never too senior to be wrong, and they're never too junior to be right." He also likes to remind new hires of a quote from Ray Dalio, investor and author of *Principles: Life & Work:* "Inexperienced people can have great ideas too, sometimes better than more experienced people."

A Matter of Processes

Legacy thinking further stymies innovation. That's what happened at India-First Life as well as at LifeNexus, the company that came up with the personal health chipped card mentioned in Chapter 3.

Both companies had innovative new ideas that could disrupt their industries. Both companies had business platforms in place. But implementation did not work out (the first time around at IndiaFirst Life) because both companies failed to embrace new processes with their new platforms. They tried to make the old, outdated processes work instead.

Just because an old process *can* operate with a new platform doesn't mean a company is optimizing its new platform. A DOM is about speed, ease, and optimization of digital capabilities in terms of your data, process, and experience.

And the Future. . .

Is yours a company that thinks innovation is for the other guys? Remember, future survival is about disrupt or be disrupted.

We all know the competitive nature of the multibillion-dollar personal products and beauty industry. So how does a beauty tools maker compete and innovate? Specifically, what could be special about a pair of tweezers? What possible innovation could disrupt the market for such a staple found in almost everyone's cabinet?

Think the outrageous, the unbelievable, the what-ifs. That's a part of innovation for the future. What about a micro-camera attached to the tweezer? Crazy, maybe. Impossible—not necessarily with the capabilities of a digital operating model.

One tweezer manufacturer considered the impossible. Sure, the innovation has its issues, problems, and drawbacks. The cameras could fall off or break; customers and consumers might not like it. But. . .what about connecting the camera to an app on a smartphone? That's innovation. It sounds a bit out of this world and far-fetched, but the manufacturer's team worked on it anyway. Unfortunately, it's an idea still a little ahead of its time. With the DOM, exploring possibilities is endless.

PRE-ASSESSMENT

Before beginning any assessment, leaders should take the time together to talk about where the company is today and visions for its future. Be sure to take notes and even create a spreadsheet for reference later.

This also is a time to discuss perceived strengths and weaknesses in the company. What are the most common customer complaints? What about staff and leadership complaints? Are deliverables and objectives aligned?

Whitsons, the culinary food group, is a family-operated company. The company's leaders sit in the same room and have lots of discussions about different departments and business processes all the time. But a closer assessment revealed that despite all the conversations, no one had a common vision for the future of the company. Once the entire family shared the same visions, Whitsons could set itself up for success.

Assessment and Evaluation

The goal of an assessment is to determine both As Is and To Be. So, it's important to analyze existing data, processes, and experience with the present as well as the future in mind. Be thorough and include not only the business side but also systems architecture and technical as in IT and other process approaches.

Also look at your competitors, their tools and their products or services. How does your company stack up? What's great and what isn't? Again, all this should be written down and added to that spreadsheet.

Finalization and the Road Map

With a thorough accounting in writing of As Is and To Be, a company now should have the beginnings of its road map to digital transformation—what's right, what's not, and goals and visions for the future.

NOW IT'S YOUR TURN TO BUILD A BUSINESS PLATFORM

Here's a quick look at how any company, any size and in any industry, can implement a thorough assessment that results in a solid digital transformation strategy and road map.

As you move through this assessment end to end, write down the results. Be sure to assess both the business as well as the technology sides of the company to determine the positives and the negatives and tackle the challenges.

This is a holistic approach in which you scan your total business with the goal of identifying roadblocks and opportunities in the business, in data, and in experience flow.

Step 1: Know your Business

As markets continue to change and companies add more products/services/ locations, it's essential to revisit a business's strategy before jumping into a digital road map. What worked in the past might be redundant.

Mapping the end-to-end business flow is eye-opening. It starts from the origin of the product or service and ends with the product or service delivery to and interaction with the customer. Follow-up matters, too.

A critical part of the analysis is knowing the number of touchpoints a customer has with the company. Also important is understanding how many departments and functions touch the process before delivery to the customer. Are all those touchpoints relevant and required?

To ensure accurate results, create a questionnaire for all the stakeholders. Start the interviews with the CEO or top executives of the company, followed by multiple department heads based on the size of the company. And don't overlook frontline workers. Equally important is to know how the frontline workers feel about business and digital enablement.

Step 2: Know the Data Flow

Once you've mapped the business flow, it's time to review data flow and determine whether each touchpoint receives accurate and quality data. That data is like blood flowing through the human body. For all things to function properly, blood must flow to every part. Similarly, data is the blood of the business ecosystem and must be able to touch all parts.

A skilled technology team is the most effective when it comes to reviewing data flow across systems and architecture. That's because most companies have a hodgepodge of data architecture as a result of a mix of legacy and newer systems that often don't or can't interact.

Step 3: Know the Experience Flow

Business flow combined with data delivers experiences to customers and employees. To truly get an accurate assessment of experiences of employees as well as customers requires a third party to conduct surveys of both.

With unbiased feedback from customers and employees, it's possible to truly understand the real output of the business.

The Next Step

With the assessment in hand, a company can build a road map that lays out multiple transformative initiatives with digital assets. Of note, however, these initiatives should be implemented over time—usually years.

It's a matter of budget as well as that prioritization of work matters the most in the short-term and then what follows in the mid- and long-term is a fundamental aspect of building your business as a platform. People involved in this exercise must know the latest tools and digital channels to deliver experiences to customers. So, bring in the experts to help; if not, these types of analysis often fail.

Parameters

You first need to know where you are so you can figure out where you want to be in the future. Nothing should be overlooked or off limits—not even an occasional nuance or complaint from a customer or employee as it relates to the three elements of the DOM: culture, platform, and innovation, or data, process, and experience.

This assessment is your opportunity to fix the pain points, create better, smoother, easier experiences internally and externally, and lay out a pathway to future growth.

Sample *To Be* Road Map: It Projects

After thoroughly assessing its current system and future needs, a financial services company wanted to map important future IT initiatives. But the company also wanted to ensure strategic alignment between corporate goals and on-the-ground business needs.

Here's how the company broke it all down.

Corporate Goals

- Increase customer focus.
- Grow emerging markets.
- Reduce costs.

Strategic Objectives

- Leverage customer insight data.
- Reorganize for global efficiency.

IT Capability Gap

- Integrate disparate ERP/employee resource planning systems in different geographical business units.
- Migrate to software as a service (SaaS) application delivery model.

IT Project Initiatives

- Implement digital onboarding.
- Implement reporting system.
- Implement robotics and automation of processes.
- Implement customer relationship management (CRM) through a software as a service (SaaS) delivery model.
- Implement invoicing system.
- Implement automation of know-your-customer (KYC) process (fraud protection standards).

PATHWAYS TO GROWTH: A ROUNDUP

- With the DOM, uninterrupted customer service can be a reality; so can seamless operations and accurate data across the board. All that comes with ease of scalability and applicable privacy and compliance rules and regulations in place.
- The transformation to digital maturity isn't always smooth sailing.
- The first step toward digital maturity is about exploring the full potential of what you have, and then leveraging those assets in the best ways possible.
- Once a company embraces the DOM, it becomes a matter of explore, exploit, and then disrupt with the power of digital.
- A crucial aspect of the road map to becoming a more efficient and effective business involves figuring the best way to utilize existing systems and assets—including people—and how to monetize them now and into the future.

- Build, buy, or rent has been a bottom-line conundrum for businesses big and small since the dawn of the digital age. It's all out there, adding to the choices available to businesses today.

- Leaders and decision-makers should approach DOM transformation with the idea that now the company, its people, and customers have the freedom to choose what they want when they want and how they want to have it delivered.

- A key component of the digital operating model is fostering innovation from the top. Executives need to foster an environment that welcomes and embraces new thoughts, ideas, processes, and approaches.

CHAPTER 7

DOM in Motion/Mid- to Large-Size Company

Insurance: Crum & Forster

"I wouldn't be able to attract great people if we hadn't spent the time establishing the culture."

—Marc Adee, CEO Crum & Forster

Level 4 on DOM

Culture: High level, decentralized

Platform: Solid ecosystem that enables fluidity

Innovation: Utilizes business process automation to innovate new ways of doing business

Crum & Forster was typical of most major insurance companies when Marc Adee took over as CEO in 2015. The nearly 200-year-old business was a top-down culture with decision-making concentrated in the home office.

A DIFFERENT APPROACH

At the time Adee and his management team began the company's transformation, they realized up front that customer satisfaction is dependent on employee engagement. "In terms of the DOM flywheel, we believe that it is our people and culture that get the flywheel spinning," says Adee. Therefore, the company's first step in the transformation was toward making C&F a great place to work.

Keep in mind that the traditional management school approach to success called for strategy first, followed by culture, execution, and people. That doesn't work in today's digitally enabled business environment. The new flow, as Adee's approach reflects, is culture and people first followed by a strong vision and strategy with data-driven execution.

More Changes

Beyond improving the basic elements of culture like physical environment and benefits, C&F focused on helping people chart their long-term career paths within the company. As part of this initiative, Adee says he thought about what he would have wanted out of the organization when he was moving up through its ranks.

One of the key—and most disruptive—changes was the move to decentralize the business units. As a result, most of the company's shared resources were pushed from the corporate center into the divisions. That move really gave the division presidents control over their destinies.

The cultural changes had a huge impact on employee satisfaction, too. Today, 9 out of 10 employees say they would recommend C&F as a great place to work. The resulting energy also was channeled externally, with C&F increasingly seen as a great business partner, says Adee. All that has bolstered top-line revenue and profit margins.

Power of Innovation

With respect to innovation and navigating the digital landscape, the move to decentralization unlocked innovative ideas and digital solutions that started bubbling up from the business units (instead of flowing downward from corporate), Adee says. "In the old days, it would have been a big decision to invest in an underwriting or claims processing system, and the decision would have been made at the corporate level with an eye toward doing the most long-term good for the most business units," he says.

"In a specialized company like C&F, this left many of the business units doing manual workarounds to process their policies. Now when you look at our more interesting machine learning, artificial intelligence, robotics process automation projects—even some of our core operating systems—different businesses experiment with different systems. They find what they think is going to work for them and try it out without having to wait in line or get multiple levels of signoffs from corporate. They can just go ahead and do it."

To keep ideas flowing across the divisions, C&F has established what it refers to as guilds—including one dedicated to artificial intelligence and machine learning—where team members can show off their new solutions to people working in other areas of the company. Says Adee, "When I sit in on the AI/ML guild meetings, I am amazed at what some of the teams are working on to improve our business. Like you say, they are making the impossible possible."

UNLEASHING THE POTENTIAL

That culture of empowering its leaders and unleashing their potential has paid off for C&F. Add to the equation the business platform and the results are transformative. Change hasn't been instantaneous, and there has been some resistance. But with culture as the driver, once change started to happen, it became easier to introduce new ways to do things.

Now at C&F it takes a few minutes to write an ordinary insurance policy or a few seconds to determine risk numbers thanks to data science made possible via business platforms. Claims can be real time and investments in artificial intelligence have helped eliminate errors as well as some of the tedious and repetitive tasks.

C&F has grown too—from $1.7 billion across its divisions when Adee took over to $3.7 billion in 2021. Looking at just C&F's Accident and Health division under its president, Gary McGeddy, 2015 sales totaled $500 million. Now they're $1.3 billion and, McGeddy predicts, on the way to more than $2 billion by 2024.

Driving Transformation

McGeddy attributes his division's growth to culture, specifically all the investment made in life and career coaching.

"Several macro elements go into building an organization that has the steady trajectory of growth and consistent underwriting profits," says McGeddy. "To me the most important thing is building a culture where you allow people to focus on achieving excellence."

"All kinds of things impact an employee's ability to perform and achieve excellence. So trying to create an environment of really high potential, high performers who are focusing on everything that they can bring to the table that's positive in their personal and career life will then create an environment where you have 20 people, then 50 people, and then 100 who are all trying to achieve excellence as opposed to just the C-suite."

Multiply that attitude of excellence by C&F's Accident and Health division's 1,000 employees and combine it with the power of a business platform and it becomes easier to understand the division's tremendous growth. "It's not just about us trying to drive the bottom line, which is obviously very important. It's about what differentiates you in market," says McGeddy.

He admits that some people may think career and life coaching is a little bit too cuddly for a major insurance company. But he says an individual who has not sorted things out at home won't show up and do their very best in the workplace. To that end, the company helps employees take care of all quadrants in their lives—spiritual, mental, emotional, and physical. If an employee is happy in all areas, that creates a culture of extreme excellence, says McGeddy.

This holistic approach is a big part of developing the right culture to embrace digital transformation today. Authenticity, trust, transparency, and vulnerability are all part of building the foundation for the future of work and business, too.

Power of Decentralization

Adee attributes the success of the decentralized approach to leaders like McGeddy who lead his divisions. "We have really great people who really flourish when they are given authority and autonomy."

McGeddy points out that if he always had to ask permission for everything, his hands would be tied, and the company's growth stifled like so many other companies that flat-line or report mediocre earnings. "I have been empowered. . .so that I can run my own company. . . . They give us enough rope to hang ourselves or achieve extreme growth."

In C&F's case it's been the latter backed by the power of the business platform.

DOM IN MOTION

C&F is a great example of what happens when a company aligns the three elements of the digital operating model triangle—culture, platform, and innovation—and high performance naturally follows.

Says Adee, "When I got here, C&F needed to evolve. We took the journey—and now C&F is a great place to work. And it has paid off in terms of attracting people—getting people to want to do business with us—and performance."

A DETAILED LOOK AT THE DOM JOURNEY

COMPANY: Crum & Forster, wholly owned by Fairfax Financial Holdings Limited

INDUSTRY: Diversified insurance product company (pet health, surety, credit, contractors, environmental, travel, trucking, commercial package, workers' compensation, property, cyber)

HEADQUARTERS: Morristown, New Jersey

NUMBER OF EMPLOYEES: 3,000

IN SHORT:

AS IS (before digital transformation). . .

Business. . .
- Lackluster results.
- Low employee engagement.
- Top-down processes/centralized control.

Technology. . .
- Legacy systems.
- Manual workarounds.
- Top-down resource allocation decisions.

TO BE (after decentralization and digital implementation). . .

Business. . .
- High performance.
- Great place to work.
- Great business partner.
- Decentralized business units.
- Ideas bubble up within organization.

Technology. . .

- Decentralized technology decisions.
- Machine learning business submission triage—allows underwriters to promptly focus on best quality accounts.
- Pricing algorithms—fueled by big data sources.
- Robotics process automation (RPA) implemented to streamline repetitive processes.

MANTRAS FOR SUCCESS

C&F leaders and technology specialists considered the following questions and solutions in helping to map their journey to digital transformation. Every company will have its own questions and find its own solutions. The important part, however, is to be willing to embrace the challenges and be open and transparent enough to search for the answers.

Some of the questions and solutions on C&F's journey to digital transformation include:

- **How do we make this a great place to work?**

  When the mood of employees—and therefore the working environment—improves, everything is better.
- **How do we take that new energy and focus it externally to be a great business partner?**
  - Smaller, empowered business units.
  - Our people are closer to the customer and need to be able to do their work in live, real-time without top management guiding their every move.
- **What is the landscape of transformation in terms of the combination of technologies used?**
  - Artificial intelligence/machine learning.
  - Robotics process automation.
  - Technology customized for different business units.
- **How can we enhance the customer experience?**

  Insurance is not a fun product to buy—but at least we can make it easier.

PART III

DON'T GET DISRUPTED

CHAPTER 8

Crisis Creates Opportunity

Resiliency is the pathway to handle the storms.

The idea of change in whatever context almost always elicits some resistance in a workplace or business. From the boardroom to the frontlines, grumblers put up roadblocks and create all types of challenges.

It doesn't matter how great the purported benefits of the proposed changes could be, there are always those people who prefer the status quo or don't like what's proposed.

Also guaranteed is that change is inevitable, as is discord over needs, wants, and what's best. So, in the spirit of problem solving, let's recognize resistance is part of the DOM journey; understand the possible resistance points and why they occur, and plan ahead.

Taking preventative actions up front can alleviate problems later. Or, at the very least they can lessen the pain points on a company's digital journey. A business should approach growth and transformation like life or death in order to have the resiliency and agility necessary to shape its future.

FAILURE IS A PART OF SUCCESS

Don't forget that failure is a huge part of innovation. It's part of success, too. Thriving companies promote cultures that accept failure as part of the experience and success as paths of disruption. After all, disruption is the beginning of the journey to add value to your product or service, and for your customer.

123

Not beginning the digital journey itself is a failure. Companies that hold out against the digital operating model aren't providing their teams internally or their customers externally a digital presence to meet their needs and the needs of doing business today or delivering the experiences expected tomorrow.

Because failure happens, incremental implementation of changes makes sense. The same goes for trying out a change with a small test sample first to determine its success potential or not. Companies—especially smaller ones with little extra available cash or people—can't afford to waste valuable development time and money on ideas that are good on paper, but wrong in real-world application.

The Pivot

Whitsons learned that firsthand. When the company began the DOM journey, its initial thinking was to distribute school food service processing at the ground level. Each elementary school would take its own inventories and place its own meal orders electronically on a tablet, says CFO Beth Bunster.

A small-scale test proved otherwise. There was some resistance from school food service personnel who weren't used to doing daily electronic input. It wasn't realistic either to assume they could do it because many of these people were older and not necessarily adapters of technology.

It was like the square peg in the round hole. As a result, Whitsons, with its agility mindset, shelved the ground-level approach and found a different way to get the needed information into the system the same day.

Concept versus Application

Though the test sample netted solid results for Whitsons, even when something works on a small scale in a controlled environment, that doesn't always mean smooth or successful adaptation company-wide.

Again, consider Whitsons. Early on conceptually almost everyone in the company liked the idea of streamlining processes and combining siloed systems into a platform ecosystem. But, says CEO Paul Whitcomb, different departments had different perspectives and different, sometimes competing, struggles ensued.

The nutrition group at corporate, for example, wanted complete control over its part of the process to ensure compliance with the extensive rules and regulations associated with institutional food and food delivery. But realistically that's not always possible in the field where unexpected variables abound.

One day a vendor might not show up at a school, forcing implementation of a backup plan, or perhaps someone vomited in the school cafeteria, prompting its closure. Those unplanned events can upset schedules and preplanning and require a quick pivot instead. That pivot calls for ground-level, not corporate, decision-making.

On-the-Ground Wisdom

That ground-level feedback is essential, not only with the journey to digital maturity, but in the context of developing a company culture primed for innovation and growth. After all, the experience is what matters today.

"The people who do the work are the ones who know what's best," says Ari Asher, of Global Furniture Group. "You just need to listen and make people believe that when you say things can get better, you mean it. Bring your ideas and let's talk about them; let's identify what we need to fix, and we will fix it together. It's not about talking; it's about doing; it's about deliverables, and it's about timelines, responsibility, and accountability. It's a team job. No one can do it on his own."

PROBLEMS AND SOLUTIONS

To better understand and address potential challenges, a company needs to think about each stumbling block as it might relate to the three common elements of DOM: culture, platform/architecture, and innovation. A company also must address how its data, processes, and experience—internally for staff and employees and externally for customers—relate. Specifically, data has a direct link to the platform; process depends heavily on culture; and experience delivers convenience through the lens of innovation.

Among the biggest challenges with the quest for digital maturity in any industry and any size company is a lack of recognition of the real problem that needs solving. Instead, companies lead with the solution.

People become so enamored with technology that they think it's the solution even though they haven't really identified the problem, says Ian Worden, a veteran healthcare IT and product executive. Typically, a business leader states the problem as something like, "We need a consumer portal."

That's not a problem, says Worden. It's a solution to a perceived problem. The real problem is the business leader wants consumers to take more or different actions and a portal is the presumed answer. Instead, spending more time and effort on defining the actual problem can lead to more effective ways to leverage a business platform and solve the problem. "The important distinction here is to establish a clear problem to be solved, before assuming the technology solution," he adds. "The business platform is a means to an end—strategy is the end."

THE IT DISCONNECT

With the onset of the COVID-19 pandemic and the need to work remotely, American Carpet South, a small New Jersey–based company that installs flooring for a big box retailer, knew it had to do something different. Its current patchwork system built piecemeal and on the cheap simply couldn't handle successful migration to the Cloud for even basic services. The system wasn't designed to be internet-based and kept breaking down, compromising data, and prompting complaints. The company's relatively new phone system wasn't reliable either.

In the Right Direction

The company had to get its system up and running now and didn't have the luxury of starting over as a first step. So, as a temporary solution, ACS minimally reengineered the system for the Cloud.

Then, the company set out to identify the real problems and design ACS 2.0—a modernized, updated, and upgraded system that could incrementally fold parts of the legacy system into the new system and help the company move forward.

Like many companies, a big part of ACS's problems stemmed from a lack of interest or expertise in IT. As a carpet installation company, management always assumed it didn't need an information technology department or specialist on staff. They figured, why spend much money on IT, and they definitely didn't have a long-term vision for the use of digital. At the time, the company was still using an outdated and unsupported operating system.

Typical Troubles

All that is typical of many smaller companies no matter the business or the industry. These businesses marginalize IT instead of recognizing its importance in building their companies to operate smoothly today and into the future. Only when a company understands the importance of IT can it learn to leverage its existing operations—explore/exploit—and move forward on the digital journey.

And as also is typical at most companies no matter their size, the various digital systems that ACS did have—like finance, inventory management, and invoicing—didn't talk to one another. They were purchased piecemeal and cobbled together.

Suddenly, amid the pandemic and forced to work remotely with its broken system, this company—as is typical with many others—realized it had to become digitally savvy to survive. It was a wake-up to the realization of disrupt or be disrupted. ACS had to identify its strengths and weaknesses, what worked and what didn't, and what it needed today and tomorrow to be successful—an assessment of As Is and To Be in terms of the business and technology.

Pathway Forward

ACS could then begin to develop a road map for the future. That step-by-step implementation guide mapped out incremental, achievable, and measurable goals on the digital journey. The assessment also is an opportunity for the company to look ahead and consider the (im)possibilities. That includes building in services and conveniences internally and externally to surpass the competition and disrupt the industry.

The small company was willing to take the lead. Now it's showing the big box stores how the job can and should be done. And, it's growing exponentially in the process. The company is doing all that with much of its legacy system, though it's been modernized.

The Right Staff

ACS started its journey by hiring the right person in the right seat so its system modernization would not fail. That meant bringing in a chief digital officer, a specialist in IT and business who understands both the technology and the business aspects of operations. That person in turn knows what's trying to be accomplished and how, and can work to bring together ideas and people and develop a common IT vision for the company's future.

Without that commonality of vision, a company wastes valuable time and energy trying to modernize its operations and systems. The result is something few people, if any, use. Or worse, the company could keep flailing without a viable and dependable system and eventually fail.

The right people in the right seat in the right structure includes the right staffing. Your people must be willing to change; we've talked about that throughout this book. We've also discussed how many older generations aren't as tech-savvy or have as technology-oriented a perspective as their younger counterparts. That's not a criticism of older generations. It's instead about individual relevance and frames of reference. Unfortunately, there's no secret formula how to convert the naysayers.

To those people who continue to reject the DOM transformation, Whitsons' Whitcomb points out that digital isn't a fad as much as an evolution. This isn't something that is going to slow down. Reality is that without embracing digital, companies face a slow decline that they don't realize until it's too late.

Remember Nokia? The once-thriving cell phone maker is a great example of what happens when a company ignores innovation and change until it's too late. The company went from selling hundreds of millions of cell phones annually to irrelevance in the market.[1]

KEEP IT SIMPLE

At the opposite end of the spectrum, beware of too much, too complex, and too fast when it comes to innovation and change. Whatever the change, that warning applies internally to your leaders and employees from the top down as well as with your customers.

Not Always an Individual Choice

When someone is forced outside their comfort zone, expect some degree of confusion. That's not necessarily the fault of the individual either. Beyond the challenge of dealing with something new, end users often find out by accident that things have changed. You visit a supplier's website only to find out there's an entirely new ordering system. Or, employees know the transfer to the new system is happening over the weekend, but when they arrive Monday morning, it's office chaos because no one can find anything.

Companies regularly fail to introduce change with the end user in mind. Nobody spends enough time and money training and incentivizing others to learn the new system. Again, that applies to employees as well as customers. We've all experienced personally or heard the grumblings about the new system and not enough or no training. It's trial by error or on-the-job training, neither of which is adequate.

Acceptance—and therefore training—is a huge part of introducing anything new. One great way to do that is to utilize champions. These are individuals who thrive on change and can quickly embrace what's new, learn about it, and then teach others.

Cross-training also is helpful. When people see the new process or system in action end to end they often are more accepting because with the big picture, it becomes easier to recognize and understand the benefits.

Accepting change also should be built into a company's culture. That way when it happens, it's not a big deal and people accept it more easily. We noted earlier how Marc Adee built that into the new culture at Crum & Forster.

But keep in mind that consumers like easy and convenient, and when a change delivers both, often it is more quickly acceptable to users.

80/20 Approach

Quest Food Management successfully ushered in dramatic digital change with the help of what its CEO Nicholas Saccaro calls the 80/20 rule. Instead of requiring his people to overnight fully embrace all aspects of the business platform model, he and his teams asked their people, "What are 20% of the features of any of these new technology tools that will allow you to be 80% better at your job?"

Saccaro took that approach, he says, because in the face of the pandemic, overnight, schools closed and things changed. People were afraid to go to work; they were afraid for their health and for their children's health. Adding to those fears, many of his people weren't technology-savvy.

"We really tried to dial back from a usage-of-the-tool standpoint because adoption was slowly growing," says Saccaro. "We said, 'Instead of worrying about being an expert in all areas of the platform, we want you to focus on the two most important parts of this platform that are really going to drive the efficiency of your operations and your ability to plan well for the next however many months.'"

That streamlining of the learning curve combined with very focused and ramped-up levels of digital, video training, and other ongoing interactions with managers and employees made a difference. The company even adopted a platform that enabled them to text every employee in the organization for messaging from the organization, what's going on, training, and more.

"Within two to three months we probably got to a place where utilizing these tools became more second nature than feeling like it was a big disruption from what our prior lives looked like," says Saccaro. "It really is pretty remarkable how quickly our folks adapted, particularly considering we were coming from the Stone Age in a lot of ways."

Incentivize Acceptance

Bringing in change managers also can help businesses encourage adoption of change. These managers work with human resource departments to create incentives to encourage staffers who are change adverse or confused by changes to adopt whatever is new. Without that type of encouragement and adoption people will claim the new system is too complex—even though it's much easier—and often revert back to the older, cumbersome ways.

It's also important to incentivize and work with customers to make sure they understand any new changes or systems. Too often customers gripe that a company sends them a new system but doesn't provide adequate training. That training should be figured into the cost of doing business, especially today in our highly competitive marketplaces.

WISDOM OF HINDSIGHT

Companies and people already well on their way to digital maturity have more suggestions and cautions to those beginning their own journey to a DOM. Given what these leaders know now, what would they do differently next time?

Strategic Fit

Too many organizations overly focus on technology features and functions at the expense of strategic fit, says Ian Worden, who has worked with a number of companies on their digital journeys.

Instead, digital journeys should be grounded in company strategies with the digital journey an enabler and extension of those strategies. Strategic alignment and the associated measures of success also should be clearly defined upfront. Otherwise, any ambiguity in company strategy can bleed into digital strategies and limit the power of what a business platform can accomplish, he adds.

Once technology vendors are at the table, there is a propensity for the digital solution to take on a life of its own. Teams become myopically enamored with the technology's bells and whistles and further lose sight of the alignment between company strategy and the value of the business platform.

Too often and in the end, teams declare victory on launching the business platform—*standing up* the platform in tech jargon—but soon are disappointed when they realize company strategy and the platform aren't aligned. Says Worden, "Hindsight has taught me that spending adequate time up-front to understand the company strategy and the expectations around how the digital platform will serve the strategy is critical. It is essential to understand what metrics are expected to go up or down as a result of the digital platform and establish the relationship between strategy and platform. A clear cause-and-effect understanding is necessary to ensure that the digital strategy and platform are developed in a manner that ensures the highest possible strategy/platform fit."

HHS

Bobby Floyd, HHS CEO, agrees on the importance of spending time to identify the real problems up front. His company has had excellent success with the digital operating model. However, Floyd says he might do things slightly differently in hindsight.

"If I was talking to myself from five years ago, I think I might say spend more time on the front end, scoping the problem out, [determining] what is the root problem, and then piloting more. In the effort of trying to be fast, I think we've failed fast but should go a bit slower."

The company spread its resources too thin to the detriment of some of its other problems, Floyd adds. "If we would have had a better up-front scope and pilot process, we probably would have pivoted and done something else."

Floyd also suggests that it's important for companies to early on determine the elements of how to measure success in terms of bringing in new technologies. There will be changes along the way on the digital journey, but understand the parameters for success first.

Whitsons

Whitsons' Beth Bunster suggests reining in the creative process early. The creative process gets lots of people to open their minds to the possibilities and that's great, she says. But going down too many roads at once can dilute efforts and waste time and money with no end in sight.

If she and Whitsons had to go through digital transformation again, Bunster says she would "put a box around the creative process" before moving forward. Start out with the big picture and the vision, but then "skinny it down" and concentrate efforts on fewer fixes at once.

Something else Bunster says she learned about software is that when implementing an idea, a team tends to look at something and say, let's add this or this, and tries to morph the processes into the set box. "You have to be open to entirely new ways to do things. Open your mind and don't try to recreate exactly what you're doing now."

Paul Whitcomb offers his own hindsight advice. "If I had to do it again. . .I think we would want to find a way to move [the transformation] at a much faster pace. Business changes and your needs evolve from when you started, so faster to market is better."

Whitcomb also says that from an innovation standpoint, he would involve more people in the experimental trial phase. That way those individuals get involved early on and can become champions with any future rollout company-wide.

Crum & Forster

Gary McGeddy of Crum & Forster's Accident and Health division agrees on the importance of getting your people on board to foster success. But, he says, there's no perfect recipe to digital transformation success. "It's not like we're baking a pie where the recipe stipulates exact amounts of ingredients."

Instead, especially with a traditional company like C&F that's multifaceted, there are lots of working parts. The transition isn't overnight or all at once, he adds.

Plus, he says, no matter what the goals or the industry, or the company, the biggest challenge is always the people. It's not the money or the investment or the time. "It's the resistance of *Homo sapiens* to change. They're insecure. They like the way things have been done. They resist change because they are insecure."

On the other hand, McGeddy says, if he were setting out on the digital journey at a startup company, he would pay particular attention to hiring. "I wouldn't hire people with legacy mindsets. I would attract talent that was forward-thinking, that had the vision of the future, and who recognize where things need to go. But that's utopia."

Global Gate Capital

Rudy Sayegh of Switzerland-based Global Gate Capital takes right hiring even further. He says the best thing his company did when it came to its digital journey was hire an outside agency to help build a road map. The agency helped identify the internal communications gaps and all the existing processes.

Beyond the assessment, Sayegh also encourages companies to bring in a champion to drive the innovation internally. And do it early in the process.

Global Gate hired a chief operating officer so that it then had two designated teams—one to secure the assessment and another to interact with the company's business partners during the transformation.

The latter is especially important for a company with mostly young people used to adopting new technology. In that situation, the challenges are not about technology adoption, but rather mapping the technology with existing business processes.

Says Sayegh, "The best way to facilitate that acceptance is if we can clearly define the business process and then map out the new business process into the technology platforms so it's easier to adopt."

Breakwater Treatment & Wellness

Breakwater Treatment & Wellness, the New Jersey–based cannabis products and services company, is relatively new to the DOM journey. But it's definitely committed to it.

The company opted to go digital because, says its President Andrew Zaleski, "We were at the point that internally we had grown frustrated with where we were as a company digitally. We knew there was more we could do to safeguard and utilize technology, but we didn't have the time to research or know what made the most sense to spend time on."

The company brought in a third party to help with the transition, and it wasn't an overnight process either. Change is a process—a journey that takes strides forwards and backwards. "You learn along the way and the journey doesn't stop," say Zaleski.

His advice to others: "Each company and team is different. You need to be ready to dedicate time and energy to this process and, as with many things, there is never a good time. But you need to make time. Understand your team to prepare for who will be able to speak to each aspect of the business and processes. You can learn a lot from all levels of the company so be inclusive of those who are on the frontlines and those managing processes."

It's exciting to see the possibilities in the future, says Zaleski.

Global Furniture Group

Like so many other executives whose companies are on the DOM journey, Ari Asher offers this advice: move faster. "If you move, you make mistakes, you course correct, and you continue."

Some in the company, he says, were slower, initially, to accept that it needed to change and then to actually change. "But if it was completely up to me and I was the only decision-maker, then I would press even harder."

"I also believe that the solutions lie within the problems in most cases. The solutions can be found within the teams, processes, the experience we already have. . ."

FROM THE TOP

Not all corporate leaders take to transformation with the agility and wisdom of Whitsons, Crum & Forster, or Global Gate Capital. In fact, sometimes founders, owners, or leaders put up resistance and create their own stumbling blocks.

When a company already is successful, sometimes leaders are unwilling to change anything and certainly aren't open to embracing new and different approaches. Rather, their attitude is that everything must already be working right, so why upset things.

Wrong mindset. Remember, disrupt or be disrupted is the mantra for today and tomorrow.

The Cash Excuse

Forget the excuse that a company can't afford to strive for digital maturity. "You have to embrace it," says Whitsons' Whitcomb. "It's not a luxury, it's a requirement."

And, yes, it's always going to be a financial push, he says. It was for his company, too. "The reality of it in this day and age, you really can't afford not do it because if you don't, you may not realize it [now], but your company is on the decline. Even if sales are climbing, as an organization you're going to be on the decline because you just won't be able to compete; you won't be able to move into the future."

Top Buy-in

Also, high-level executives may sign off on a project but then choose to not get involved in its implementation. That's one of the reasons a decade ago the United Kingdom's initiative to bring shared services to higher education failed, according to Steve Butcher, the British education leader. A leader who simply says, "Go make it happen," isn't enough.

At the time of the attempted change, the top leaders wanted it, but as the project was passed down to various levels in the university system it went nowhere slowly, adds Paul Hopkins, the IT specialist. And it was eventually scrapped.

At the other end of the spectrum, transformation has been extremely successful at the University of West London (UWL) because, as Adrian Ellison pointed out, the school's vice chancellor buys into the importance of IT and the quest for digital maturity.

GETTING TO THE NEXT LEVEL

Figuring out how to get to the next level certainly isn't unique to UWL, the university in Leicester, or their fellow universities and companies. In these pages we've talked about lots of companies and some of their struggles to move forward on the DOM journey.

Even companies that make it look easy today faced their own struggles early on. The first steps are the hardest, says Whitsons' Beth Bunster. That first year of implementation was like going from 0 to 100 miles per hour in one shot. It was a rough year rolling it out, but the company stuck with it because they knew they needed it. There was internal resistance from some people; that's expected.

With Whitsons' outside people, too, there were a few hiccups. When the company started its digital journey, computer adoption was not as broad as it is today. The typical school cafeteria "lunch lady" might never have used a computer before and, therefore, was a bit hesitant.

But Whitsons knew it had to change and so it did. The company used a phased approach to implementation that mostly worked well. There were a few bumps, but the company worked to get the right people in the right jobs to make the transition happen.

"Now," says Bunster, "it's business as usual. The only thing we have to control now is we are so dependent on software, our users want more. We have more asks now than we can ever do."

REGULATORY STUMBLING BLOCKS

Implementing a digital operating model is doubly difficult in the healthcare and finance fields, IT veteran Ian Worden says, because, like food service, both industries are heavily regulated and come with strict compliance standards that must be a part of any innovation and adoption of technology.

In the healthcare field, cultures also are very entrenched. Consider that today's largest user of the fax machine remains hospitals![2]

Also, clinicians are evidence-based in their thinking while digital innovation often is hypothesis-based. That dichotomy doesn't always lend itself to adoption of the latest and greatest technology, Worden adds. That doesn't mean innovation can't or doesn't happen. It simply takes longer.

However, there's evidence it can get better. The quest for and discovery and development of the COVID-19 vaccinations is a great example of what happens when the power of technology and brainpower come together without restrictions to solve problems. The impossible is possible.

SECURITY CONCERNS

Any discussion of challenges linked with digital change must include the issue of data and system security. Older, patchwork systems simply don't have the protection capabilities of a streamlined platform ecosystem.

Important Protections

That's especially important today with rampant ransomware and other malware. One coffee company, unsure about digital in its future, was forced to scramble after a ransomware attack ended up costing the company the $20,000 paid to its attackers.

The company had to pay up to protect its and its customers' data. Following the attack, the company decided to upgrade and modernize its system and now has multiple layers of protection as well as a strong firewall and a defined security policy that limits access.

Think of your data and your system like your home. You don't give your house key to everyone and you don't give system and data access to everyone. Conversely you don't go away for the weekend with your front door wide-open. Companies shouldn't do the same when it comes to their data and systems.

Privacy Complexities

Increasingly, companies and customers recognize that the ownership and security of data is an important part of the digital business model. That's not just in terms of who can access what data, but for what specific purpose, too.

After all, among the advantages of a business platform ecosystem is the ability to analyze and leverage data in real time.

But, as mentioned earlier, even though many younger generation consumers relinquish their data all the time via social media, its usage and privacy issues remain a gray area. In the healthcare field, for example, a health plan or provider may have captured customer consent for data usage; however, how the data is manipulated as it relates to data ownership isn't always clear, says Worden. "There was a time when you could de-identify data, scramble, and mix it up to create data outcomes. Today, however, we are obligated to build new software solutions that utilize synthetic data. Then all data is perfect to your specs and that's not how data comes in."

Some other things to consider when it comes to system and data security include:

- **The importance of multi-factor authentication.** It's essential, not only at the user level, but also at the system level. When a user is profiled in the system, what is their level of access and why? That should be spelled out in detail.
- **Continuous system vulnerability.** No matter any product or organization's assurances, no system is 100% secure. How is your company protected from ransomware?
- **Backup protection.** Almost every company has some type of system backup, but is yours enough? It should be thorough, frequent enough to meet your company's needs, and easily accessible.

PATHWAYS TO GROWTH: A ROUNDUP

- Thriving companies promote cultures that accept failure as part of the experience and success as paths of disruption. Disruption, after all, is the beginning of the journey to add value to your product or service, and for your customer.
- Among the biggest challenges with the quest for digital maturity is a lack of recognition of the real problem that a company needs solved. Instead, too often companies lead with the solution.
- Companies need to take the time up front to understand and align strategy and expectations around the business platform.

- Support for digital maturity across all levels in a company is an important part of successful transformation.
- There are plenty of excuses why not to embrace digital maturity—including, "We can't afford it." But companies today can't afford not to if they hope to remain competitive.
- Older, patchwork systems do not offer the security and protection capabilities of a streamlined platform ecosystem.

CHAPTER 9

Outsmarting the Competition

A business platform modeled after the shopping mall helps companies quickly capitalize on market share.

Today's consumer behaviors are changing faster than ever, creating new opportunities and threats in the process. Those companies with their houses in order—their business platforms on track—can proactively meet these demands and challenges faster and will come away the market-share winners.

Platforms offer the necessary agility for swift changes as markets dictate. They also foster the platform effect—user numbers snowball as services increase and more users tap into the system. The bottom line is that DOM in motion can be the pathway to outsmart the competition.

Whitsons is a great example. As mentioned earlier, the company and its technology partner worked for more than three years to roll out their initial business platform, but only three months to roll out a subsequent enhanced product to meet changing market needs. That's the competitive power of the business platform.

DISRUPT OR BE DISRUPTED

History is full of stories of once hugely successful companies that failed to transform quickly enough and ended up extinct or nearly that way, says CP Jois, a longtime global CTO. Retailers Kmart and Sears once had stores everywhere; today they're down to a handful. The once-omnipresent Toys "R" Us is another brick-and-mortar stalwart that's disappeared—though more recently it's been reborn online.[1]

Vine, an app enabling users to post six-second video clips, once disrupted the competition. It was bought by Twitter and touted as the next big thing. Six years later it was outsmarted by more competition, including Instagram, and finally shut down.[2]

Brick-and-mortar booksellers Borders and Barnes & Noble were equally outsmarted by their competition—Amazon, which began as an online bookseller. While Borders and Barnes & Noble each initiated their own online presence, for Borders at least, it was too late. More importantly, their online presence wasn't executed as well as Amazon, with its deep insights model, says Jois. Borders closed its doors in 2011 and Barnes & Noble was bought out and taken private in 2019. It continues to struggle.[3]

Disruption begins with outsmarting the competition, says Jois. But, no disruption happens overnight. It actually occurs as a series of outsmarting events. "Cumulated over time, the damage is done."

THE SCIENCE OF BUSINESS PLATFORM AND DATA

Crucial for any company to stay ahead of the competition is the data science and analytics provided by business platforms. After all, data is the commodity and figuring how to monetize it becomes the differentiator. It's back to the shopping mall analogy as a recipe for data monetization. That's when a business organizes data with integrated processes to deliver experience on any device.

Speed of Reality

Companies used to rely on (long) past data behaviors to predict future outcomes. In our fast-moving digital world that's no longer enough. Now the true differentiator—what can help a company rise to the top and go beyond—is data behavior and digitally enabled data science.

You don't know what you don't know—seriously! Data science proves that. Data science combines data collection, analysis, and intelligence to extract information on behaviors and provides more effective outcomes. In tech jargon, it's extracting data patterns with the goal of creating or making an intelligent experience. With data science, companies can quickly identify once-hidden patterns and potential in real-time.

Instead of waiting weeks, months, and even a full quarter for trend data collection and analysis that's already outdated, a business platform and its digital ecosystem can crunch the numbers and the data real-time for nearly instantaneous results. Those results enable company agility and swift change implementation as markets dictate.

Whitsons used to have to wait weeks for data and trend analysis; so did C&F, ACS, and so many other companies. In the beginning, the University of West London didn't have the data in the right format either. Now all these companies, with their digital operating models in place, can perform quick data analysis as part of their standard operating procedure. Better still, with the data that their digital ecosystems provide, outsmarting the competition not only becomes possible, but probable again and again. And, once you know the data well, it can be monetized multiple times.

Now, Whitsons knows almost instantly when a process or procedure falls short and can change or tweak it as necessary. That means less food waste, fewer wasted work hours, more personalized and better experiences, and most importantly happier employees, happier customers, and happier customers' customers.

And, at HHS, as discussed, the data is easily available and provides a clear picture of operations and shortcomings.

Knowing More

The most important aspect of getting ahead and staying ahead of the competition is to do things better, says CP Jois. To do that, one must *know* more. With that deeper and better knowledge, we're then empowered and can do better.

All this segues into the fundamentals of insights and intelligence. This is also where the concepts and constructs of machine learning and artificial intelligence begin to take practical shape. Knowing more about a customer, client, employee, or investor enables a more targeted approach to delivering value. The paradigm shifts when an enterprise changes the value equation from generically focused to hyper-targeted.

Even if two competitors provide the same service, combining targeted value with targeted pricing strategies makes a difference, says Jois. As simple as it sounds, too often performing better than the competition comes down to the more subtle aspects of a sale. Product and price usually have been cast as the dominant characteristics. Reality is that more subtle aspects can be effective elements to outsmart the competition. The simplicity of approach, pricing transparency, consistency of customer experience, speed, and agility collectively change the competitive ambiance.

Focus Internally

Andrew Zaleski and his company, Breakwater Treatment & Wellness, know the right way to outsmart the competition in the highly competitive cannabis industry. "We try to focus on ourselves and not what others are doing," says Zaleski.

Instead of comparing and competing with others, Zaleski and his team believe in the quality of their product and in their business model. After all, if a company and its people don't believe in their own product, how can they expect their customers to do so?

Breakwater goes above and beyond for those customers, whether it's about educating them about their products and services, improving the shopping experience, or personalized service. The strategy is paying off, too. Despite many other cannabis companies in close proximity, Breakwater's customers drive up to 45 minutes for the experience.

NEWEST EVOLUTION

Outsmarting the competition through disruption certainly isn't new—not even in the digital space. Remember the Palm and later PalmPilot, once so dominant in the handheld, personal digital assistant space that its name was synonymous with hand-held devices? It was outsmarted by the competition—smart phones—and faded into oblivion.[4]

Another famous collapse—Sports Authority, which had more than 450 stores across the United States—went from $2.5 billion in sales in 2005 to shuttered doors and its intellectual assets sold for $15 million to its biggest competitor, Dick's Sporting Goods, in 2016.[5]

Then there's Kodak of camera, film, and failure-to-evolve fame. The company finally accepted the idea of digital pictures too little, too late.

The evolution to data science is the next disruption. It's not so dissimilar from the transition to change we discussed earlier—from the traditional ROI dollar-for-dollar return on investment—compared with the new ROR, the rate on return and investing for dramatic multiple returns.

It's a new and better way of looking at doing business with future survival and growth in mind. It's maturity in the AI (artificial intelligence) space with more detailed and unique analytics. And, it's back to the idea that you don't know yet what you don't know. And you didn't until now, thanks to data science. The answers come from extracting the meaning from the data structure and organizing it in an algorithm to create multiple outcomes.

Beyond Simple Data

This new way of thinking and doing with today's data science marries data with emotions and intuition to reveal the big picture. The result is a vibrant company that can react quickly to the changes and needs of its people and its customers.

Utilizing data science, a company can have real-time inventory management that ensures products are available when they're needed. No more incidents of a plane not flying due to the lack of availability of a small part; or the car production line at a standstill until a single part can be located. AI-powered inventory management can even make sure the corner coffee shop isn't out of your favorite flavored coffee.

Additionally, with the help of a digital operating model, data science capabilities can be unique to every company and among individuals. That's an ideal approach because every scenario differs for every business and person. All processes, for example, are not the same for everyone. Individual methods, cultures, and behaviors differ. Data science recognizes that and in real-time can factor all that into calculations, analysis, and conclusions.

Then, aligning those differences with the data creates layers of intelligence that can help companies take the right steps to better understand the product their consumers want and outsmart the competition. The bottom line is an intelligent company that makes decisions based on intelligent information and choices.

The Wild Card

With all this intelligence, data, and direction, outsmarting the competition can happen. But it happens only if a company has embraced innovation and isn't afraid to try something new that changes how things have always been done.

Higher education is an expensive and very competitive business, especially in London, where nearly 400,000 students study at about 40 institutions.[6] Among the biggest challenges these universities (and others) face is attracting new talent and retaining students and the revenue they generate.

As mentioned earlier, to improve its users' experiences and outsmart the competition in the process, the University of West London decided to embrace a unified platform ecosystem. Before, UWL—and its competition—operated primarily on legacy systems that generally required multiple log-ins to access various services—from library information and access to finance, student life, and more.

Plenty of money was at stake. At UWL, for example, one student equated to more than £9,000 of income for the university each year. That's more than $12,000. Losing one student meant the loss of nearly $50,000 over a four-year period.

UWL's unified platform system provided its staff and students a smoother, better experience back then. Now and into the future the system continues to evolve. When the university decided to up its student-retention game, the platform's data science and analysis capabilities were front and center. "This wasn't UWL going out and saying let's do some analytics," says Adrian Ellison. "Rather, we had a business problem to solve."

Initially, UWL partnered with an outside technology vendor and rapidly deployed its analytics platform. Now the university can track real-time the latest student enrollment, attendance, and dropout trends. That enables the university to tweak its offerings, scheduling, staffing, and services to gain a competitive edge.

Next, UWL decided it wanted to track every time a staff member reached out to a student to encourage and help with engagement. These interventions, though, weren't back-office analytics. These were "in your face analytics," says Ellison. So, once again, in line with the university's agile and caring culture, he and his team went to the students to make sure they were comfortable with using these analytics. The result was an analytics policy coauthored by UWL's student union.

That effort resulted in a rise in student completion rates, from 76% at the outset of the program to 85% in just four years, says UWL's Peter John. "That's an example of how we can use technology to adapt to the problems we face rather than be servants to them."

This across-the-board support and implementation separates UWL from many organizations. Says Ellison, "The reason analytics worked for UWL is the chancellor backed it to the hilt and we got the whole organization behind it. Analytics is not an IT project; it's a business transformation project that IT is helping to deliver at the backend."

DELIVERING TO CUSTOMERS

As UWL so aptly demonstrates, outsmarting the competition in any business is all about delivering better experiences internally as well as externally to customers.

Christopher Yin, a global creative director, recounts the story of a leader in the premium coffee machine market who wanted to improve its brand experience and disrupted the market in the process. The company offers high-pressure brewed coffee, espresso, cappuccino, and latte machines that retail for $799 and up to thousands of dollars.

Since design is a key attraction of its product, the company capitalized on the potential of a DOM and introduced augmented reality (AR) to the selling process. Now, potential customers simply use a smart phone to scan a QR code on the company's website and they can see a specified machine in their personal environment (more on the technical aspects of the process later), says Yin. Wondering what a machine might look like next to the toaster on the counter, or perhaps worried it might not fit next to the refrigerator in the break room? No problem. Thanks to the app, the customer now sees and knows ahead of time.

The purchase process means less guesswork and more a real-time reality. Customers end up with fewer concerns and, therefore, a more pleasant shopping experience. That's the power of an intelligent user experience with augmented reality—intelligent data aligns with intelligent front end for an intelligent user experience. And all of that is part of the intelligence economy, the recipe for outsmarting the competition.

DEVIL IN THE DETAILS

On a grander scale, multinational finance and technology behemoth Mastercard also counts on a digital ecosystem to expand its markets and grow exponentially.

Inter-country transactions—known as cross-border transactions—traditionally have been extremely complex and laborious operations that can take days. They're further complicated by financial rules and regulations that differ vastly by country as well as regions, states, districts, and localities.

Consider a transaction between the United Kingdom and India. Each country's central bank is different. So are each country's clearing and settlement requirements that must be followed exactly. In other words, manually clearing and settlement between different countries can be daunting. With multi-rail (card, bank account, blockchain/DLT) digital platforms, it's a different story—one that makes the process quick and simple.

To be successful, these operations must be one step ahead in terms of understanding the jurisdictions and regulations as well as recognizing the individuals involved. Even better, it's a system that has the flexibility to instantly adopt to changing rules and regulations. Plus, the system is built to scale. When the demand for services is greater, no problem. The system takes it all in digital stride.

Marketing Piece of the Puzzle

Consumer behaviors have transformed so businesses need the DOM now more than ever for the flexibility and management connections that a digital ecosystem provides. The new world is about influencers marketing along with product information management (PIM) and reviews.

Today before someone shops or dines, they likely check out reviews, read about products, or learn about them from independent resources. Some products or places, for example, could suddenly be the latest and greatest because an independent reviewer shared an experience real-time on Instagram.

That doesn't mean knowing and understanding your markets, and marketing what differentiates your product or service, aren't part of the path to outsmarting the competition. Rather, the key is how you approach the marketing.

With data analysis capabilities built in, business platforms enable companies to continually understand evolving consumer trends in real time and stay a step ahead in terms of knowing what the consumer wants.

A large British direct-to-consumer (D2C) company created D2C websites, not to boost sales, but to provide real-time data on how their messaging affects consumer purchasing. The company ultimately failed because its marketing technology was too complex. With the power of the business platform, companies already have access to that real-time data and can react immediately to customer messaging and preferences.

When it comes to marketing your product and service to outsmart the competition, when it's better, smoother, faster, and easier, consumers, customers, and customers' customers notice. It's not the competition that matters; it's giving consumers what they want. And your business will grow from there, says Joe Santagata, CEO of ACS.

Listen to Your Customer

Companies also have to pay attention and listen to the needs of their potential customers. That means understanding the demographics and how they relate to what you want to do, where, and why. No matter how good a product, if a potential customer doesn't need it, want it, or won't use it, it likely won't sell no matter the amount of marketing.

Consider a digital payment product, for example. India's population is young and demands the latest technology. Therefore, it makes sense demographics-wise to introduce a digital payment product there that can and likely would disrupt the market.

Name Recognition Matters

Brand recognition also can contribute to outsmarting the competition, especially when it comes to introducing and gaining acceptance of changes to processes and procedures. Consumers familiar with a brand are more likely to take changes—including digital upgrades—in stride.

Mastercard is a master at that kind of consumer acceptance, too. The technology behemoth's logo is everywhere at sporting events worldwide and on social media. Chances are most of us at least once have heard the advertising phrase "Start something priceless."

MORE CHALLENGES, PLATFORM SOLUTIONS

Virtual reality seems to be taking to the next level everything from journalism to football, and retail training. The NFL and some college teams use VR as part of their player training.[7] News outlets including *The New York Times* and *The Guardian* as well as some broadcast channels also are looking at how immersive technology can enhance coverage.[8]

Not long ago a big-box retailer introduced virtual reality as part of its employee training and development program at its training facilities. The program was so successful, now the company is providing Oculus VR headsets to its U.S. stores to elevate training to all its more than one million associates.[9]

Digital Onboarding for Employees

Typically bringing on new employees—onboarding—is a time-consuming and exhausting process for companies and their already-stretched-thin workforces. Over the years the hiring process has evolved to online applications as standard operating procedure.

But company onboarding hasn't always been as quick to latch onto the digital model. That could be because an employer still wants the human connection; they simply haven't kept up with technological changes, or a combination of both. Whatever the reason, competition today demands a new employee hit the ground at full speed. Technology enables that.

Faster Background Checks, Screenings

HHS hopes to take that digitalized onboarding a step further and outsmart the competition in the process. Because attracting enough labor is so tough, HHS's Bobby Floyd and his team are hoping technology can facilitate faster onboarding so that his company can draw on a larger potential labor pool.

The problem for HHS is that unlike many other businesses looking to hire unskilled labor, the healthcare field has time-consuming rules and regulations that must be followed. That includes preemployment screening and extensive background checks even for the simplest jobs.

"If I'm a cook or housekeeper or transporter and looking for a job, Walmart can hire me in three days," says Floyd. "Whereas in the healthcare environment it will take three weeks because of rules and regulations."

If someone needs a job quickly to pay bills that are due, that slower-to-hire company will lose that potential employee. "That's why we're looking into technology to automate that onboarding process," he says.

GAME CHANGERS: AI AND MACHINE LEARNING

Artificial intelligence and machine learning already enable all kinds of companies to disrupt the competition and it's only the beginning. Streaming services count on machine learning to make viewing suggestions; social media feeds and chatbots use machine learning;[10] financial institutions look to machine learning to identify potential fraud; and machine learning as a service and machine learning operationalization are taking off in the IT infrastructure and services industry. With the latter, companies can better predict expected incident volume and provide better, quicker, and smoother resolution of IT problems.

Explaining the Differences

However, AI and machine learning are not really interchangeable. Let's clarify some of the terminology.

Artificial intelligence (AI) is simply intelligence exhibited by a computer/machine as opposed to a human. **Machine learning** (ML) is a type of artificial intelligence in which a machine can learn and become smarter on its own. In other words, the computer learns without the knowledge being input by a human.

Combining **data science** with machine learning nets **automated machine learning** (AML), which removes humans (and their ingrained biases and opinions) from the equation. The **internet of things** (IoT) adds internet accessibility (like a smart phone) to the equation and makes devices all around us intelligent. For example, with IoT, a coffee machine can have the ability to hold data and communicate with other platforms. Suddenly, usage skyrockets.

AML in Action

Automated machine learning is gaining popularity in the insurance industry when it comes to determining creditworthiness, risk assessment, and mitigation. For example, instead of asking potential policyholders lots of questions that can skew outcomes depending on the answer, insurers look to automated machine learning. These platforms examine vast amounts of data—financial as well as personal and more depending on the type of insurance or policy— for patterns and anomalies that can be flagged, and then allow for specific explanations.

The coffee machine maker earlier in the chapter counts on three-dimensional product visualization and augmented reality (AR) to market its products. The company knows that customers expect this enhanced experience. Like Best Buy, the company also recognizes traditional photography, regardless of angles or clarity, can be deceptive and is outdated as a method to display products digitally on a website.

With its unique approach to product display, the company provides potential buyers a realistic 3D picture of the product in their own space from all angles. The 3D model shows scale and interacts with the environment's lighting. It's a virtual beyond-the-in-store experience at home.

This digital-try-before-you-buy creates a better consumer experience and outsmarts the competition by leading to increased engagement. It also helps a potential buyer answer questions such as, "Does the machine look right or does it fit in the intended space?" This kind of user experience engages the customer more often and longer, and ultimately can lead to more conversions. The use of AR also reduces the probability of product returns and provides a significant reduction in overhead.

The University of West London uses automated machine learning to help identify and cut down on potential student dropouts. With dropout rates, the challenge always has been how to detect student disengagement before dropout occurs. With automated machine learning in play, early warning signs are visible months ahead of time. Those disengagement signals include student action points like access to assignments, library use or lack thereof, class attendance, and more.

With the data gleaned from a unified platform, a student's learning can be more individualized to their needs, including intervention when necessary to help someone who is becoming disengaged, struggling, and a potential dropout.

There Are Limitations

Before conjuring up images of machine learning taking over the world, keep in mind that machine learning—like most other technologies—isn't for every situation. That's because not all tasks are suited for the technology.

ML also raises certain ethical issues. Should we trust an algorithm instead of our own judgment? Matthew Stewart, a data science expert studying at Harvard University and an AI consultant and blogger, points to some of these ethical and data issues in a blog on the limitations of ML.

"Algorithms allow us to automate processes by making informed judgments using available data. Sometimes, however, this means replacing someone's job with an algorithm, which comes with ethical ramifications. Additionally, who do we blame if something goes wrong?" Stewart writes.[11]

PATHWAYS TO GROWTH: A ROUNDUP

- Business platforms help companies roll out products faster to stay relevant and capture the emerging needs of consumers.

- Today's consumers aren't as concerned about how great a product or service is. But they do want to know how and why their lives can be made easier with new processes, products, or services made possible with the DOM.

- Companies must pay attention to the needs and wants of their potential customers. That means understanding the demographics and how they relate to what a company wants to do, where, and why.

- Artificial intelligence and machine learning are game changers when it comes to disrupting the competition. Intelligent data combines with intelligent consumer channels (mixed realities) to create experiences that enable companies to outsmart their competition.

CHAPTER 10

DOM in Motion: Business Platform Success

Digital maturity: When a company fully embraces the culture, platform, and innovation of the digital operating model and is ready for what's next.

Meet Mastercard 2022, a digitally mature global technology giant that continually innovates and integrates the latest in industry platforms, behavioral data, and Cloud and mobile solutions into business and financial institutions' processes for a better, more secure customer and consumer experience. The company is an excellent example of the three elements of the digital operating model triangle—platform, culture, and innovation—working together, continually to evolve the company, its accomplishments, and its growth.

Other companies mentioned in previous chapters, like Whitsons, University of West London, Global Furniture Group, HHS, and Crum & Forster, are well on their way to digital maturity, too. All these companies embraced the digital operating model and at various levels continue to work hard to leverage all that it can offer their businesses, their customers, and their customers' customers. The future, after all, is about making life better and easier. Growth follows.

PLATFORM POWER

It is no longer whether companies can develop or utilize the latest technology. Most any company can do that today. Rather, it's all about the user experience.

Companies that are digitally mature or well on their way understand that and are the leaders in creating the best experiences. True end-to-end business platforms deliver the power and potential to maintain the momentum necessary for the DOM in motion.

"It's not just about the money we make," says Joe Santagata, CEO of ACS, the flooring installer. "It's more about one of our core values, 'Do things for others the way you want others to do for you.' I think sometimes in business, people forget that."

DISRUPT OR BE DISRUPTED

Adrian Ellison of UWL, along with his peers at other companies that have embraced the digital operating model, firmly believes the mantra "disrupt or be disrupted."

Companies can disrupt from within, developing their own platforms, processes, and innovation. That's how companies like HHS, Whitsons, and Crum & Forster got started on their disruptive journey.

For other companies, the disruption can come through acquisitions. That's how Mastercard disrupted.

THE MASTER

Many people think of Mastercard as primarily in the card space—servicing one payment rail, as it's known in industry jargon. The Purchase, New York–headquartered technology company is a leader in the global payments industry, providing a multi-rail offering and touching hundreds of millions of lives in the process.

Mastercard is a prime example of a digitally mature, Level 5 company engaged in exploring and disrupting in the twenty-first century. And, in turn, the company delivers on data, process, and experience. The company utilizes the power of the digital platform ecosystem to leverage data, deliver on processes, enhance customer and consumer experiences, and enable digital and financial inclusion for millions of people worldwide.

Prime Acquisition

That's especially true after Mastercard's 2016 acquisition of UK-based Vocalink, which powers key payments technology platforms in the United Kingdom and elsewhere.

A few of those technologies are:

- Bacs Payment System: the Automated Clearing House (ACH) that enables direct credit and direct debit payments between bank accounts.
- Faster payments: real-time account-to-account service enabling payments via mobile, internet, and telephone.[1]

With that acquisition, suddenly, Mastercard had the platforms and the power to disrupt, and it did.

At the Forefront

In the past decade, the rise of real-time payment systems as an alternative payment rail posed a potential threat to the card retail payment model, says Paul Stoddart, Mastercard President of New Payment Platforms. "Mastercard's approach [at the time] was to say that there are certain aspects that could be disruptive and so we are going to ensure that we are going to disrupt ourselves, and that we are developing and really understanding a robust approach to that challenge. We wanted to ensure that we are a part of it rather than it being done to us," says Stoddart.

"The acquisition of Vocalink was very much about ensuring that Mastercard was participating in real-time payments, retail, and B2B flows over real-time payment systems, which were very much considered the main disruptor for card payments," adds Stoddart.

As a digitally mature company, Mastercard continues to innovate and diversify its businesses to embrace all the payment rails that exist today and ensure that it's participating in the development of new rails.

Says Stoddart: "Initially that means expanding electronic payments coverage to account-to-account payments. These represent over 80% of all electronic payments. Card payments represent less than 20% so it makes absolute sense that Mastercard should want to participate in all payment flows and payment types. In doing so it means that we can be the payment partner of choice for many of our customers whether they are banks or corporates.

"We don't want to have increased complexity, and so participating in all flows and being the partner of choice enables a simpler, more efficient engagement model with our customers and we believe back for our customers with us."

Forward Spin

Looking ahead, Stoddart says that distributed ledger technology or digital currencies also represents an emerging rail and funding source. Just as there are account-to-account transfers from bank accounts, there would be a blockchain network and a crypto- or digital currency.

"As that new rail and that new emerging payment ecosystem happens, we feel we need to be part of that and can bring the experience, the expertise, the capabilities that we've developed over the years for the other rails to that rail," he says. "Primarily it's about engendering trust between participants."

Partnerships and More

Beyond its initiatives under its own name, Mastercard provides services to other payment system operators across the globe. Again, it's all part of the company's financial inclusion agenda that brings the power of digital to the fintech space.[2]

With Mastercard's pledge to connect a billion people to the digital economy at the forefront, the company enlists partnerships and co-collaborations. A few of those initiatives include:

- Strive, a global initiative focused on strengthening the financial resilience of small businesses and supporting their recovery and growth. In Thailand, Mastercard provides the technology underpinning Prompt-Pay, a national payment system that also enables the Thai government to distribute benefit pay to citizens and reduce fraud in the system.
- The Strivers Initiative, a consumer-facing platform, elevating the visibility of Black female business owners overcoming obstacles to maintain and grow their business, as role models for the community and future generations.

"We absolutely believe that the most effective approach in the digital economy is to embrace a combination of a sort of direct and indirect channels to market and engage with our customers," says Stoddart.

He also points to the company's efforts in the merchant retail payment space. That aggregative approach enables hundreds of thousands and even millions of businesses to accept payments via Mastercard. As a consequence, these intermediaries extend Mastercard's ability to reach many more customers than it could directly.

Next-Level Engagement

Mastercard brings its digitally mature, innovative, and disruptive spirit to the next level of engagement, too. The company enables both direct and indirect customers to engage with its technology around all its various payment rails—to consume, test, trial, and self-serve.

"Our developer platform becomes a place where potential customers are partners. They can go and look at and find the directory for all the APIs [application programming interface] we have that would allow them to access a range of services. I think it is a way to bring our customers closer. Rather than keep them at arm's length and engage in a more standard formal and sequential process by opening up our developer platform and our APIs, this enables customers to come closer to us to be able to avail themselves of the services we have to offer in most cases without any human interaction and in a more dynamic way," adds Stoddart.

Cash Constraints

Disrupt or be disrupted is the mantra. But despite Mastercard's size, its reach, and its innovative agenda, the company still faces a familiar challenge for almost all businesses, especially those not already heavily focused in the e-commerce arena.

That challenge is funding its initiatives—getting the balance right between funding new product development and innovation and growing and maintaining existing revenue streams, says Stoddart. The COVID-19 pandemic put a lot of pressure on large businesses to constrain their funding of new product development initiatives because of the reduction in revenues.

Most businesses that had a significant element of their business dependent on areas of the economy impacted by the restrictions around COVID-19 have had to scale back their funding on innovation and new product development. Mastercard is in that same situation, says Stoddart. "Not remove it; just constrain it" until revenues return to normal and then grow again.

"Whereas before we may have placed maybe ten more speculative investments in innovations, we will now only place five but that's still a meaningful reduction," he adds.

Initially, the University of West London worried about financial uncertainty, too, when COVID-19 slammed the world in early 2020. "We were all thinking, will we have any students at all?" says Ellison. So, the university made what he says were some "harsh decisions," and cut its innovations budget at the time.

But, because the students kept coming and recruitment remained very strong, UWL was able to eventually invest more in its cutting-edge UWLFlex, a mix of online and in-person learning. While still maintaining tight control on its finances, the university did, however, continue to make strategic investments and grow as a result.

SIMILAR CHALLENGES

As is the case with UWL, just because a company doesn't have massive scale or reach doesn't mean it doesn't face some of the same challenges.

The cost of digital transformation worried Whitsons, too, early on and ongoing. By 2022, the big concern was the rising costs of goods that the company must deal with every day.

"We are going into a market right now with hyperinflation, in some cases up 100%," says Whitsons CEO Paul Whitcomb. "I'm not sure how technology can help there, but doing what it does to keep tighter control over the numbers puts us in a better position."

Touching Lives

Along with many of the companies mentioned in these pages are other local, regional, national, and international companies that have embraced the power of the business platform and improved the lives of their people, their customers, their customers' customers, and their bottom lines in the process.

All are on the journey to digital maturity and working hard to deliver on better, faster, and more streamlined experiences. The power of the business platform helps solve one problem, and then with a little tweaking we can solve a bigger problem somewhere else, says Bobby Floyd, CEO of HHS. His multinational hospitality company has grown exponentially since embracing the DOM. After the first five years, HHS doubled in size, and then doubled again over the next five years.

At one point the company even considered monetizing its digital model—selling the tools it developed internally to improve operations. But then the company opted to keep it proprietary. "We feel it's our competitive edge," says Floyd.

IndiaFirst Life embraced the DOM and brought the digital mindset to end-to-end insurance services for its customers. The University of West London utilizes automated machine learning to help students stay in school.

Global Furniture Group uses the business platform to streamline internal operations and deliver better and more consistent services to its clients.

Each of these companies innovates in its own digital way. They operate on a scalable business platform, leverage data, process, and experience, and deliver better, faster, and easier to their people, their clients, and their clients' clients. They stay relevant by delivering greater experiences, and they're not done yet.

"Constant investment in automated processes and digital infrastructure is required to stay relevant," says C&F's John Binder. "If this is ignored, one can't simply write a large check a few years down the road to catch up. It requires constant investment and innovation as well as an agile technology planning process to road map the future but constantly update with the latest information."

Crisis: Lack of Skilled Labor Pool

As constraints on the labor pool become more apparent, HHS hopes to streamline its backend system to facilitate multiple diverse operations for the same company on one communication platform. Right now, for example, the company may provide food service, operations and maintenance, transportation, and cleaning services to a single company as siloed operations. Combining them all on one platform is the future, says Floyd.

It's all about explore, exploit, and disrupt and the ability to optimize your people and services to provide a better experience.

Floyd says his team could consider investing or participating with companies that are disruptors within its supply chain and that now are a cost of doing business. For example, he says, HHS might look at how it can use its company as a platform to help these companies grow. That doesn't necessarily always mean an exchange in capital either. It could be as simple as using a company's product—a field test, for example—in exchange for an equity stake or share of the company.

Regulations: Checks and Balances

Like HHS, Whitsons isn't yet at Level 5 of digital maturity, but it also has bigger and better plans for the future.

As is typical for companies at this level, Whitcomb looks ahead. He's not concerned about the competition as much as he is unexpected, sudden changes in the market, particularly regulatory changes that he knows well can happen overnight, such as in 2010 when Whitsons faced massive market upheaval with the passage of the Healthy Hunger-Free Kids Act.

In the financial services and technology space, Mastercard faces regulatory challenges, too. In part because of the vast differences in operating in certain spaces and countries, Mastercard will partner with local domestic operators or license its proprietary platforms in some countries and areas, says Stoddart.

Undaunted and Undeterred

Change is the constant for the digitally mature. In today's hypercompetitive, ever-changing markets if a company isn't moving forward, it's falling behind.

Beyond the platform and various payment rails and partnership initiatives, Mastercard is innovating from within. In 2021, the company brought product and engineering under one umbrella to help break down the silos that exist between business lines. Previously, the teams were split as product, sales, and then operations and technology.

The goal was to create a much more integrated products and technology capability to increase speed and response to customer needs, says Stoddart. "Twelve months into the journey and already it's showing strong signs of success in our ability to respond to customer needs more effectively."

Overcoming Legacy

Making changes and eliminating silos isn't easy for legacy companies, including Mastercard. Most every company struggles somewhat, whether they are in insurance or food service, healthcare or education. Even small companies struggle with trying to change entrenched ideas, processes, and cultures.

It's a struggle newer companies without older ways don't face. Those companies born in the internet age more naturally adopt that sort of approach, says Stoddart. "Fintech startups now don't know any different. As a consequence, they almost certainly will have an advantage by doing everything digitally and electronically with very limited or zero manual or paper existence. That's a world that is very different than when you were setting up a business 10 years ago."

Small businesses today don't have many of the entrenched barriers to change common to companies like Mastercard. "That's part of the challenge for businesses that have been around longer—how to engage with and indeed compete with businesses that don't have to worry about how to transform, that don't have to worry about how to get more efficient and manage a very complex technology estate," says Stoddart.

It's an interesting psychological element of freedom that fintechs benefit from and puts larger businesses at a disadvantage. "Hence the need for the transformation," adds Stoddart.

And when it comes to disrupt or be disrupted, Whitsons' Whitcomb says, "If you're not doing it, someone else will."

High-Impact Presence

Every company is unique and their pathway to DOM different. Yet, the issues and challenges they face aren't all that different.

Global Furniture Group's Ari Asher has worked for diverse companies, from technology to now office furniture. "Over the years I changed industries because I was always curious about what's out there," says Asher. "I really enjoy learning."

When he first came to GFG, everyone kept telling him the company was unique and therefore its operations and challenges unique and not necessarily suited to the changes he advocated. "Every place is unique in a way," says Asher. "But no place is really unique because at the end of the day it's all human nature and everybody is doing the same thing. Some people are doing it a little bit better; some people can improve. But at the end of the day every place I have been is the same. The same issues that we have in the furniture company, I had a few years ago at a technology company."

Those companies and their leaders who recognize that and understand the benefits of digitalization will find success now and in the future with a DOM in motion.

PART IV

THE FUTURE IS HERE

CHAPTER 11

Maintain Your Forward Momentum

The future revolves around the intelligence economy
powered by the intelligent business platform.

The future of work, we all know by now, is the digital platform. Throughout these pages you have learned how various companies and industries are embracing the digital operating model on their journeys to digital maturity.

Hopefully, you also have a clearer picture of how a digital operating model with its interconnectivity and ease of use can continuously fuel this evolution to improve our lives and build new pathways.

With a digital mindset, we are in alignment to embrace the future of work. That future revolves around collection of data at the front lines rather than the more traditional C-suite, top-down decision-making. Humans will learn more about what they really need to solve specific business challenges and machines will become smarter to deliver better experiences.

Moving forward, faster, and easier are the mantras of this digital age. A better experience is what digitally savvy companies strive to deliver.

But what happens in the post-digital era? Who will prevail? What technologies will make our lives easier? Whatever the answers to those questions, the evolution of business will continue to happen with intelligence and automation.

Ultimately, though, the computer, no matter how intelligent or how it's used, is a tool that's part of the human experience. And because humans create these machines, computers won't outpace us—at least not likely in our lifetimes.

INTELLIGENT BUSINESS PLATFORM

The intelligent business platform lays the framework for businesses to be future ready. In today's world AI makes data intelligent; robotics and automation make process intelligent; and consumption via any channel—voice, meta, mixed reality, and more—makes experience intelligent.

When all three combine, a business becomes intelligent, says Dhana Kumarasamy, global CEO and digital expert. Future generations will expect this kind of hyper-personalization delivered smoothly so that any business acts as one platform offering consumers everything the business has available.

To deliver that kind of experience requires future-ready businesses to map their customers and company's complete products and services, and to engage with the market through the latest channels. That's the path to gaining market share, adds Kumarasamy.

HYPER-PERSONALIZATION

Hyper-personalization happens as machines learn more about us and data becomes more descriptive. And it's all with the goal of delivering a better experience to the end user.

Personalization is central to information delivery based on the context, personal preference, and profile-driven information for consumption. What makes it hyper is the experience that makes life better, more meaningful, actionable, and sustainable, says Kumarasamy.

Hyper-personalization has moved from information consumption to an integral part of an individual's decision-making. No longer is it necessary to search for your interests. With hyper-personalization, the information already is delivered to you in your context.

"With digital evolution today, multidimensional information can be collected and curated in real time from many sources. Those sources are connected devices ranging from our intelligent vehicles to watches, security cameras, information banks, commercial establishments, schools, and governments. Then, combined with deep learning/machine learning and AI, they offer capabilities for contextualization without any static input or instruction. This truly empowers people to make the right choices and experience in the given situation and context," says Kumarasamy.

For example, someone could design a shoe based on their feet, physical activities, body type, foot/heel structure, and weight. The system then could process all this information automatically, and the AI engine develop the shoes, choose the materials, and manufacture the final product using a 3D printer. Such is the power of an intelligent business platform.

HUMAN AND MACHINE

Before we look closer at more specifics of the future, let's take a step back to understand the similarities between humans and computers and the role of intelligence in the equation. Then it's easier to see the potential.

Data Gathering

Arguably, a child is born without intelligence. That's similar to the basic hardware that is a raw computer, also without intelligence. Humans collect data over time as they grow; computers collect data over time by interactions with consumers and the use of the platform.

Humans have two sides to their brains: left for analytical and right for creative. Computers have two types of data—left data and right data or structured data and unstructured data.

Structured data is the organized data used in our systems. Unstructured data is all over the internet with or without our knowledge. When both types of data combine, the two become *big data* and can be monetized with the power of the business platform.

Rather than roll your eyes or reject the term *big data,* consider this: prior to computers, then-massive amounts of information—data—were stored in files and piles of paper. Back then no one ever called it *big paper,* says digital data expert Yuri Aguiar, author of *Digital (R)evolution: Strategies to Accelerate Business Transformation.*

Of course, the millions of reams of data on paper pales compared with the massive amounts of digital data that's generated today. In 2019 alone, internet-connected devices (internet of things/IoT) generated 17.3 zettabytes (ZB) of data (1 ZB is 1,000,000,000,000,000,000,000 bytes—that's 21 zeros). That number is expected to top 73 ZB by 2025.[1]

Turbocharged

Aguiar, Chief Enterprise Data Officer at London-based The WPP Group, likens monetizing big data via digitally enabled data science to a car's turbocharger. Most data—80 to 90%—that companies generate is likened to exhaust that's not being used. With a car's turbocharger, exhaust is recycled to create an extra boost of power. "What we are doing is recycling this data or turbocharging it," says Aguiar.

Digital platforms also can analyze unfathomable amounts of unstructured data to find patterns far beyond the capability of a human or even a group of humans. In tech jargon, combing through all that data translates to the capability to find *cognitive elements out of dynamic data sets.*

Aguiar recounts an experiment in which an AI bot—a robot equipped with artificial intelligence—and a human watched the same video. The bot came up with 63 facets or descriptors that the human couldn't even fathom. "That tells me there are patterns in things that we as humans just can't identify," says Aguiar.

Companies that do not invest in their data capabilities constantly must adapt or react, says Aguiar. That's inefficient and sets them back in most competitive business arenas. On the other hand, dynamic and visionary organizations make this strategic decision and stick with it, which leads to greater operational efficiency. These companies also are far more likely to be innovative in their businesses.

Data versus Intuition

That's not to discount intuition in corporate decision-making. Both data and intuition are tools available to companies and their leaders to make better decisions and drive better experiences for all participants.

Plus, sometimes what some people might think is a crazy idea isn't really and is the impetus that brings about change. When cofounder and then CEO of rideshare service Uber Travis Kalanick brought in surge pricing—paying more at peak times or when driving is difficult—people railed. But the company stuck to its guns and dynamic pricing is the norm today.[2]

The best decisions are those that are a combination of data-driven and intuition. For example, as discussed earlier, in higher education, machine learning (ML) can identify the early warning signs of a student becoming disengaged. Then, with trend data in hand, a counselor can make an informed decision on how to move forward to best help a student.

It's much the same with ACS, the carpet installer. CEO Joe Santagata relies on digital-reliant data science to analyze real-time data so that he can manage by leading indicators, not lagging ones.

The same happens at HHS. When its people have leading data, they can make better decisions, says CEO Bobby Floyd. In healthcare settings, for example, turning over a hospital room for a new patient is labor-intensive and often occurs amid a rush of additional patients. With platform-generated data, hospitals can now predict these rush periods and increase efficiency. That avoids backlogs and can eliminate patient delays.

Human Potential

In other words, data science complements human brainpower. We all have heard the myth that humans only use 10% of their brains—in reality we use all our brains to some extent.[3] Whatever amount of brainpower we as humans do use, computers and data science can fill in the shortfalls.

And, when untapped human brainpower and computer intelligence combine, they become a superpower that has the capacity to make the impossible possible. That's digital maturity and the continuation of the never-ending journey to better, faster, easier. Exponential growth follows.

But keep in mind that data is just data, says UWL's Peter John. "Data gathers; it doesn't let you do things with it, and it doesn't have impact. You have to use it to be constructive, innovative, and different," he says.

When It Works

Information and its quality certainly work as an asset for HHS. Floyd points to a community gateway system that it has developed for an acute-care hospital. In the past, collecting the right referrals and identifying hospital vacancies as part of the patient admissions process was extremely cumbersome and usually required multiple staff telephone calls.

Now, with the help of a digital platform that HHS and its partners developed, doctors and medical teams within the hospital's system of care have direct visibility to vacant beds. That's streamlined the referral and admissions process to the point that medical professionals prefer the ease of using the hospital's system over others in the area. That's boosted patient numbers and bottom lines in the process.

The digital platform works so well other area hospitals that initially weren't part of the rollout now want to be included on the platform. It's a win/win/win for everyone—including HHS—in terms of data, process, and experience as well as financial gain.

The Tesla vehicle is another business platform that disrupted the market, but not in the way many may imagine. Tesla isn't an electric car; it's a great example of an intelligent business platform—a software platform inside a moving iron box.

The car is the experience channel. Data and process control its movements. A "driver" holding the wheel is the experience.

FULL POTENTIAL

More people and companies have begun to realize that information/data is yet one more tool to help a business achieve its full potential. But, very few, if any, businesses actually operate at their full potential consistently. Even those companies that are digitally savvy, embrace the digital operating model, and count on data science for an edge still struggle to maximize their potential. Widespread use of artificial intelligence is not yet the norm for companies.

That's often because the more we know, the more we grow, and the more we seek to rise to the next level. There's always more to learn and more that can be accomplished. Once technology enables us to answer one question, we have so many more, and we want so much more. It's back to, *you don't know what you don't know. . .*until you know it.

Looking to the future, many business executives say they want to work harder to further leverage their platforms and do a better job at helping their businesses achieve their full potential. Many point to data science, artificial intelligence, and machine learning in an intelligent business platform as future keys to gain that competitive edge.

TODAY IS HERE

The future already is underway. For those who doubt the extent of how digital already affects our lives, thought leader Aguiar suggests we think about a typical person's ordinary day. People's lives already revolve around the intelligent platform.

Digital Connections

The number of digital connections we already rely on regularly can be mind-boggling—from data points to apps, to visual and voice elements, big data analytics, and beyond. Says Aguiar:

I wake up in the morning to the alarm that I've set on my phone for the entire month. My coffee already is brewed thanks to instructions input on my smartphone and conveyed over the internet to my smart coffee machine. I get in my car to drive to an appointment and my digital assistant, with its British accent, reminds me to "buckle up."

I plug the address of the appointment into my GPS, which relies on satellite uplink and downlink connections to guide me. Driving to the appointment at 60 mph, I'm on a hands-free conversation with someone in Australia. As I drive, the call bounces off various cell towers and I'm automatically being billed for my data usage as I talk. Once at my destination, I stop to make a lunch reservation on Open Table, after checking out the app's suggestions for nearby restaurants. And, when I'm in the elevator, I check the score of last night's New York Giants game.

That is the reality of my life. By the time I get into my office, I've already consumed from about 1,500 data sources.

This is likely your life and that of most people at most companies around us.

The Numbers

Still not convinced ours is a digital world and it's time to embrace the platform? Consider just one aspect of the digital footprint: voice-activated devices. On a planet with about 8 billion people, there will be 24 billion voice-enabled devices by 2023. At the same time, the number of devices with digital voice assistants (like Siri, Alexa, Google, and so on) will top 8 billion, according to Statista. That's up from 3.25 billion in 2019.[4]

With 24 billion devices, we have to believe they're reaching all markets everywhere, says Aguiar.

Data Science Insights

Already big data seamlessly connects us to make our lives easier. Aguiar, who regularly travels from Long Island in New York to the same Florida destination, recounts his regular routine:

- *A rideshare company from his Long Island, New York, home to John F. Kennedy International Airport.*
- *A Delta Airlines direct flight to Fort Lauderdale.*

- *Pick up a rental car from Hertz at the airport.*
- *The return to Long Island is the reverse—Hertz to the airport; Delta to JFK; and a rideshare to Long Island.*

All these data points—Aguiar's experiences—connect in the background. The business platform has learned something about him and uses that to analyze his patterns and make suggestions. Aguiar is a Delta frequent flyer and belongs to Hertz's affinity club. As a result, whenever he types his membership number into Hertz or Delta online, related advertising, suggestions, or information that fits with his habits and interests pop up.

If Aguiar suddenly changes his travel routine—perhaps flying to Atlanta or stopping at a restaurant for Italian food en route to JFK—the platform analyzes the changes and modifies its deliverables to him accordingly. This is hyper-personalization in action.

INTERNET OF THINGS (IoT)

Delta and Hertz count on the internet of things (IoT) to deliver Aguiar (and millions of other people) the targeted ads and information. IoT basically involves combining artificial intelligence with smart devices connected to the internet.

The beauty tools maker mentioned in Chapter 6 was ahead of its time with its attempts to utilize IoT to develop a smart tweezer with a built-in nano-camera. The innovative idea was that users would be able to physically see through their tweezers via their smart phones. On the other hand, the coffee machine maker successfully uses augmented reality to provide its customers a better experience. Taking a photo on your camera is only two-dimensional. But with augmented reality, the consumer can move all around the product and see it from all angles.

Growing Market

In 2021, estimates pegged the number of IoT devices in the world at more than 31 billion, up from just 7 billion in 2018.[5] That's nearly four times the total population of the world.

An accurate estimate of the future reach of IoT is tough. Let's just say tens of billions more devices will be in use tomorrow. Companies could invest a total of up to $15 trillion in IoT by 2025.[6]

The size of the IoT global healthcare market alone is forecast to grow from nearly $61 billion in 2019 to $260.75 billion through 2027. That market growth (a 19.8% compound annual growth rate—CAGR) is fueled by growing focus on patient engagement, patient-centric care, growth of high-speed network technologies for IoT connectivity, and the growing need to control costs in healthcare.[7]

On-Demand Services

Data logic and experience are front and center in the fitness business with two popular systems, Peloton and The Mirror. Both offer variations on IoT-powered boutique fitness classes in your home. Peloton utilizes various self-manufactured fitness equipment like treadmills and bicycles with internet-connected instructors. The Mirror provides the virtual fitness assistant literally in the mirror as you exercise.

Both are business platforms with data that deliver and gather intelligence. The more intelligence gathered, the smarter the system becomes in the form of predicting or suggesting the next "class" or fitness routine. This automated machine learning reflects the power a platform brings to data science. After all, data science predicts what does not yet exist.

That same logic applies in the medical field to smart or intelligent hospital beds from makers like Hillrom, recently acquired by Baxter Technologies. With internet connectivity these beds enhance patient care by connecting patient needs and actions remotely with caregivers.

CHANGE IS INEVITABLE

For ACS, the future isn't as much about disruptive new inventions as it is about using data analytics to disrupt the status quo. The carpet installer is focused on building and enhancing its digital ecosystem of different digital tools to work better together and grow the company in the process.

Enabling Consistency

Joe Santagata, the company's CEO, wants growth for ACS, not only in size as in numbers—his personal goal is to double his business—but also in consistency with technology as a driver. He points to fast-food giant McDonald's. The chain is deliberate and even maniacal in its operations. Even the simplest things are done the same every time and in every location. It's a culture and a replicable model, says Santagata.

If with the help of AI that consistency can be replicated at ACS, then, he says, he can spend his time working *on* the business and growing it as opposed to working *in* the business, constantly problem solving on day-to-day issues. For example, on the customer service side, AI can provide valuable analytical insights.

Traditionally, if ACS has an issue with a customer, they pull phone call records and data from the system. But with the help of AI, the company can extract data before it becomes a problem, Santagata says, and do more to help people more consistently.

Innovative thinking and use of platform-generated data can end up a value add for companies. Perhaps in the future a company like ACS could develop an innovative technology or use of a technology and end up supplying value-added goods or services to other companies. After all, smaller companies are much more agile than the large behemoths and can pivot more quickly with market demands. Those companies can more easily take the lead with the help of digital operating models.

Transparency and Control

Said Hathout of Bahrain-based Al Hilal Life sees on-demand self-service and transparency as big value-adds that his industry can deliver to its customers with the help of business platform technology. That means potentially a policyholder could have full access to their policies and the ability to make changes without the need to go through a very long process to change even one small thing, says Hathout.

The concept of renting life insurance during specific activities or for a certain period of time—like travel insurance, for example—versus owning the policy is another potential option, says Hathout. "I'm not talking 10 years in the future, but maybe next year."

Though life insurance is usually a difficult product to sell because of its complexities, technology—as in the business platform—can make these various options possible.

Gary McGeddy of insurance giant C&F also sees an on-demand, digitally enabled future in his industry. Perhaps like instant payment platforms deliver fast cash, there could be an instant travel insurance payout system that delivers on the promise of money back to consumers in their time of need.

Let's say someone's plane has been delayed three hours. If that person bought a travel insurance policy with a travel-delay benefit, at three hours and one second their benefit would appear in their checking account.

That's the utopia of travel insurance, says McGeddy. But that also will become table stakes as consumers demand it.

"We owe the consumer the promise (of payout), so why do we make them fill out the form? That's the legacy process in place," says McGeddy. "(Right now) to go to that type of purely virtual environment is wildly expensive and a huge investment of time."

But, he says, "We have to pay attention to what it is people demand as consumers." That includes ease and access.

BLOCKCHAIN

Blockchain is next-generation technology. It's a special data structure or database that holds information in a decentralized environment. Each transaction is recorded in a block that's chained together with other blocks. New data means a new block, and all are held in chronological order in a way that makes it very difficult to change or edit.

It's the technology behind the Bitcoin or cryptocurrency craze. It's also considered a secure environment to hold medical records, vote tallies, and other information that needs to be trusted. So much has been written about blockchain and cryptocurrency that we'll simply provide a bit of the basics here.

An Ecosystem

A simplistic way to look at blockchain is it's a software platform, a community, and an ecosystem that is made up of a chain of records stored in the form of blocks that link together chronologically and aren't controlled by a single entity. The blockchain creates a trust based on cryptography, decentralized databases, and consensus mechanisms.

Blockchain is the next step toward disruption, says Cesar Castro, Founder and Managing Partner of Escalate Group, and a digital transformation and disruption expert. After Internet 2.0 comes blockchain, and it is allowing innovators to capture economic value in open ecosystems, he says.

When the internet happened decades ago, it was about making information and communication available anywhere without the use or need for paper. Now with blockchain, we're enabling the Web 3.0, adding trust to the mix so anyone can send digital property and digital value to anyone, anywhere. Web 3.0 is creating the incentive structures required to solve the world's biggest problems, says Castro.

The blockchain has enhanced smart contracts—contracts written in code that are executed automatically without human intervention. It's secure, and because it's immutable, the records can't be changed or tampered with, says Castro. It's a decentralized community with protocols behind it and centered around absolute trust.

Ultimate in Security

Blockchain is a public wall that provides the ultimate accountability and transparency, says Rohan Sharan, a recent graduate of Indian Institute of Technology (Kharagpuru, India) and a digital entrepreneur. Sharan is an advocate to bring innovation and disruption into the marketplace with blockchain and through cryptocurrencies like Bitcoin (*bit* is the monetary value and *coin* is the money).

In finance, for example, there are certain recording requirements that traditionally involved paper. Blockchain replicates the nature of the paper trail but brings it into the digital world with a permanent, unalterable record, says Sharan. Block history cannot be deleted so there's traceable ownership. Theoretically it also removes the middleman from transactions, removing extra fees in the process.

Peer-to-Peer Payments

Cryptocurrency, specifically Bitcoin, originated as a way to deliver peer-to-peer micropayments—electronic cash—via the internet. Blockchain is the neutral ledger for Bitcoin (and other cryptocurrencies) to be issued. Every 10 minutes the chain is extended with a new block added, says Sharan.

Cryptocurrencies are traded via decentralized digital transactions on online coin exchanges utilizing blockchain technology. That compares with the more traditional trading of financial assets on highly regulated financial exchanges like stock markets. There are literally hundreds of cryptocurrencies that are traded or mined (in the jargon) today.

New Reality

"What we have is a marketplace for computer transactions to happen worldwide," says Sharan. "All data, all transactions happen on the public blockchain, so instead of private databases like Facebook and Twitter, connectivity happens by default and at minimal or no cost. Users own and control their own data that's all stored on the public blockchain."

Already, blockchain technology's accuracy and broad accessibility is such that it can enable confirmation of transactions without a centralized clearing authority. That can expedite and lower the costs on currency transfers, corporate transactions, even voting.

Castro predicts that soon this decentralized protocols approach will move to social networks—it already has but remains niche. With the power of blockchain, individuals will maintain ownership of their information and the value they create.

This will happen in most industries, says Castro. And very fast, too. Already it's happening in the finance sector, though it remains somewhat complicated for the average user. "All this will become simpler and only grow," he adds.

MACHINE LEARNING AS A SERVICE (ML AS A SERVICE)

Just like software as a service (SaaS), machine learning as a service in the IT space will grow in popularity, too. These chatbots with ML algorithms built in can reduce human interactions. For example, banks have chatbots that, based on the questions someone asks, provide answers. Someone can open and close an account, for example, without human intervention.

Students considering attending a particular university could visit the school's website to look for certain courses. An intelligent chatbot with ML built in could draw conclusions about the student based on the questions asked and the order of the questions. The bot could then even send out an application as well as determine the potential student's level of interest and forward all that information to the university. The student can even be admitted to the university without a campus visit. An intelligent university platform also will deliver data via virtual reality that can immerse someone in the campus experience and replace or complement the university admission process.

DEEP LEARNING

Deep learning is the next step in machine learning in which the computer—the platform—becomes smarter *and* can draw conclusions without human intervention as it collects and analyzes more data.

Wrong Conclusions

With basic machine learning, a bot can learn to return better information incrementally with limitations. But it still can draw wrong conclusions that require human interface to correct. For example, someone makes the statement, "It's raining cats and dogs." A bot with ordinary machine learning capabilities assumes the literal translation—cats and dogs are falling out of the sky.

However, when deep learning capabilities are added to machine learning, the algorithm can figure out the real meaning—it's raining hard outside. It's this deep learning that has the ability to totally disrupt.

Power of Disruption

A mainstream use of deep learning is language and dialect recognition and some advanced chatbots. For example, if we ask a smart phone or smart speaker, "Show me restaurants with spicy food in my neighborhood," that's the voice-enabled experience model at work. Or, if we call for an airline reservation, the moment we select one option, we get more and related options.

Though the computer learns as it progresses, today it's only the beginning. This is deep learning in the toddler stage. There's not the ability yet to generate enough data to guide consistently accurate direct interaction without human intervention.

ROBOTICS AND AUTOMATION

As discussed, software robotics (RPA) or bots (robots) are powered by the business platform and employed to handle usually repetitive tasks. RPA, for example, can reenter the same data in multiple places almost instantly and with near 100% accuracy. The same work performed by a human could take hours and be subject to high levels of inaccuracies like missed numbers, transposed numbers, improper entries, and more.

Timesaver

HHS, the hospitality organization, capitalized on RPA with its business platform and slashed its data error rates, freed a number of employees for more creative work, and saved money in the process.

Bots also are used widely in interactive chats as part of customer service, bank reconciliation, generating reports, and in hiring. With the latter, these automated systems initially sift through and weed out unqualified candidates. Then with new hires, the bots can enhance training and cut down on the tedious filling out of lots of different forms.

As more companies embrace the digital operating model, more will look to RPA to solve data accuracy and other business challenges. That includes inventory distortion—out of stock and overstocked merchandise that amounts to $1.8 trillion worldwide annually. That's more than the gross domestic product of Canada! Potentially bots, with more accurate inventory counts, could dramatically curtail some of those losses.[8]

Limitations

But robotic process automation today still has limitations. In insurance, for example, RPA can bring speed and accuracy to analyzing risk for a basic pet healthcare policy or travel insurance.

But, to assess and write a $25 million umbrella policy is more nuanced and requires a more complex and personalized approach. Perhaps tomorrow intelligent RPA will change those limitations.

Better Experience

The labor shortage is very real, says HHS CEO Bobby Floyd. "And, I'm not 100% sure it's a function of the COVID-19 pandemic. I think there is a portion of the workforce that is not going to return."

That realization has prompted Floyd, along with other chief executives, to explore what tasks can be successfully completed with robotics. Robotics makes sense, Floyd says, because labor is not available, or if it is, it's very expensive. Plus, as the costs of labor go up, the costs of robotics are coming down.

That presents a great option with one big caveat. "What we have learned the hard way is that the technology isn't really there yet," Floyd adds. "It's come a long way . . . but we have found in some cases when we purchase robotics and we hear feedback, our people spend more time managing the robots than themselves. Using the goofs, though, as learning experiences, it will get there. It's come light-years from just five years ago."

Remember the network effect? That's the proven concept that as more people turn to the business platform, recognize its value, and begin to demand that value, the use of the platform grows. It's all about tapping the potential of technology to make our lives better. And the network effect will only grow into the future.

The cryptocurrency phenomenon is a great example of the power of the platform and the network, and how as its advantages spread more people demand and expect the value it offers.

LOOKING AHEAD

The future of technology and business is all of the above—from IoT to data intelligence and voice-activated systems to 5G (the updated, faster, fifth-generation broadband connectivity), blockchain, hyper-personalization, and more.

As more power is needed, quantum computing will deliver as it evolves. What now takes a day will take literally seconds tomorrow with the speed of quantum computing. Not based on chip technology, quantum computing is 1,000 times faster than current mainstream technology. With this technology we'll be able to analyze the entire internet in a fraction of a second. Imagine the application in business—the ability to micro-analyze massive amounts of data. Nano analytics, perhaps.

Early version quantum computers now are used by NASA for galaxy simulations and can even simulate the Big Bang. It's worth noting, however, that no matter how fast or how thorough the technology the goal will remain about the experience.

With technology advancing so rapidly, all things are possible, says Ian Worden, the healthcare and IT product executive involved with cutting-edge digital change. It's just a matter of time and money. "With that guiding principle in place, we can avoid being overly enamored with technology and instead focus on the value equation of deploying technology," says Worden. "Organizations should identify competitive differences to create value for their customers knowing that technology can be leveraged to accelerate and enhance those objectives. It is less important to know which technologies and more important to know how value is created. With clarity on competitive advantage and value creation, technologists can then help identify the most suitable existing, new, and emerging technologies to meet the need."

Looking to future and planning for the University of West London, Peter John offers an insight that extends well beyond the university setting. "The world is changing and not just from COVID, but from AI and other technologies. The students are changing; the environments are changing;

governments are changing; and the world is changing. So we have to adapt to it and modify it at the same time, which is very difficult to achieve."

PATHWAYS TO GROWTH: A ROUNDUP

- As humans learn more about what they really need to solve specific business challenges and machines become smarter to deliver on those needs, so will our experiences become better.
- The computer, no matter how intelligent or how it's used, is a tool that's part of the human experience. And because humans create these machines, computers won't outpace us—at least not likely in our lifetimes.
- The intelligent business platform delivers exceptional experience with the power of hyper-personalization.
- Widespread use of artificial intelligence is not yet the norm for companies, but achieving automated machine learning is.
- The future is here. Think how voice-activated technologies and the internet, along with big data, already seamlessly connect on demand to make our lives easier.
- Blockchain, the technology behind the Bitcoin or cryptocurrency craze, is next-generation technology. It's a special data structure or database that holds information in a secure environment.
- Deep learning is the next step in machine learning in which the computer—the platform—becomes smarter *and* can draw conclusions without human intervention as it collects and analyzes more data.

CHAPTER 12

The Decades Ahead

"True North" is delivering happiness to consumers' experiences with the power of the intelligence economy.

The future is all about unleashing the potential of businesses, people, and the devices around us. All are becoming connected with data to create an intelligence economy. In these pages you have seen how the digital operating model can power these connections to improve our lives. Companies and people that embrace digital provide their people, their customers, and their customer's customers with faster, easier, and more streamlined experiences.

FUTURE LEADERS

Looking ahead to the end of the decade, companies that lead in technology also will lead in revenues, profits, and growth. Many of the mega-corporations that used to be cutting edge in the past, but fell behind due to lack of agility and speed, may finally catch up and end up back on top.

Some of these companies likely are the market leaders of 2010 and 2020 that we discussed early on. But don't count out the digitally savvy innovators just yet. Disrupt or be disrupted is a strong mantra and motivator for innovative newer companies with great ideas (innovation), solid platforms (digital maturity), and the right culture that embraces explore, exploit, and disrupt.

There are all kinds of predictions from analysts and experts as to who will be the market leaders by the end of the decade. Will technology companies take over the world? Will giant behemoths like once-market leaders be back on top? Will Amazon, Alibaba, Google, Microsoft, or even Walmart control the world?

Speculation is rampant. But before we speculate further in these pages, let's look at some of the workplace trends going forward. Then, as technology gurus (or not), we can let our innovative imaginations take over and think about how impossible, out-of-this-world ideas can be made possible by the end of the decade.

MAKING THE IMPOSSIBLE POSSIBLE

Times have changed. So have demographics, consumers, markets and marketplaces, work and workplaces. Tomorrow will bring even more change.

A massive storm is on the horizon that has the potential to disrupt and even wipe out the unprepared. Those unprepared are the companies of all sizes and in all industries that don't embrace the power of digital.

Purpose Matters

After all, digital leads to intelligence that delivers experiences that result in happiness. That's a pathway to becoming a business with purpose. The latter is table stakes for the future and the ticket to exponential growth.

With changing demographics, markets, and even climate change, next-generation workers and consumers are passionate about sustainability and making the world a better place to live and work.[1] That drives businesses to mature their products and services and align them with a purpose.

As this book is written, new industries are evolving—in energy, space, technology, agri-tech (the marriage of agriculture and technology), crypto-finance, and many more. Product delivery methods are changing, too. Instead of owning products, people will rent them and pay based on usage, not just in terms of software. Already, today scooters, bicycles, and even small cars are available online or via kiosks. Sign up on an app on a smart phone or at a kiosk, pay online or with a card, and head out without owning or renting from a brick-and-mortar store.

Different Demands

Millennials and Gen Z—Generation Alpha is up next—are the new work-forces and consumers. Gen Z (those born 1995–2009), already 2 billion worldwide, by 2030 are expected to make up 34% of the workforce. This is the generation known as "dot-com kids."[2] Their likes and dislikes are different from earlier generations, and they will create what they want to consume. They connect via digital and engage on social media. Many will not own cars or houses; however, they will consume the latest and greatest tools that give them experience—and it must be digital.

What matters to them is visual, voice, and mobility. They constantly search for new channels to deliver experiences. "What's in it for me" could be their new mantra.

Generation Alpha comes next. These are children born since 2010 and shaped by the twenty-first century. To refer to them as digital natives is an understatement. Nonetheless, they are the consumers that tomorrow's businesses must learn to attract, engage, and market to.

In these pages we've shared how the digital operating model helps companies create an end-to-end platform. That platform then enhances delivery of products and services through a usage-based model that can quickly pivot with market needs and demands. All that is essential to meet these future needs of business. Hyper-personalization will be the norm as newer generations expect businesses to offer them what they need, when they need it, and via easy, smooth channels.

CREATIVE SOLUTIONS

With digital platforms and digital cultures in place, some companies will innovate by purchasing disruptors. That's especially true with larger companies that may not have the agility or the desire to disrupt on their own.

Disruption

HHS is one of those companies considering looking at smaller companies that are disruptors within their supply chain. Mastercard already did it with its 2016 acquisition of Vocalink, an innovator in the electronic payments ecosystem.

In the case of Mastercard, with the Vocalink acquisition the company was able to differentiate by expanding into more payment rails. One of the reasons that digital disruption could happen so smoothly for Mastercard was the company's culture. The company had the dynamic people and the vision as well as the agility to embrace the changes already occurring and on the horizon.

As discussed, that's often not the case with huge legacy companies and their entrenched ways. But, as Mastercard so aptly reflects, if any company

any size has the basics for growth and change embedded within its culture, it's much easier for their people internally to accept the change and the company to continue to grow.

Workforce

As staffing becomes increasingly more difficult in a COVID-19 and beyond world, some companies continue to look at alternatives to accomplish certain tasks. HHS is one of those companies also looking for solutions that involve less dependence on frontline human capital.

"We'd like to be potentially more involved in providing robotic solutions at the site level," says CEO Floyd.

Already, robots are in demand at many warehouses worldwide. Through the end of the decade AI and robotics will eliminate some jobs, but they will create others.

Reassigning and reskilling will be necessary, as increasing demands and different skills are needed. That requires a workforce with the right culture to embrace change, learn, and grow in the process—a crucial element of the digital operating model.

MANTRA FOR THE FUTURE: DIEP

Think of the future of business in terms of DIEP. That's an acronym for:

> → Digital
> → Intelligent business
> → Experience results in consumer happiness
> → Purpose transforms lives

Digital powers the intelligent business platform, which delivers experience, helping businesses to stay on a purpose-driven path.

In the next iteration—beyond the current digital era—data will be omnipresent and businesses will evolve through intelligence and automation. The resulting intelligence economy will rely heavily on data science and deep learning.

Data science will enable different types of data analysis, including descriptive analytics based on current or historical data; predictive analytics that look ahead; and prescriptive analytics that suggest actions based on available insights.[3]

Unleashing Business Potential

Business platforms output data. How companies and people use that data and intelligence to make money goes on. Yet there's still so much more untapped potential. It's like standout athletes who push the envelope to become better and better at what they do.

Think U.S. football legend Tom Brady or Argentine Lionel Messi, of soccer fame. They bring much more than their physical prowess in their sports to their games. They take a holistic approach, focusing on food that helps them stay fit, and mental exercises to enhance their minds on the field.

Never Ending

Bigger, better, faster are goals. And when we hit one goal, as humans we set even higher goals. Before digital, what could literally take days or months now can take a few seconds or less. Remember the comparison of *big paper* versus *big data* in the last chapter.

In tomorrow's intelligence economy, calculations, analysis, and delivery will be even faster. Algorithms may literally predict and provide without a user even asking, thanks to deep learning capabilities. Those platforms will be able to analyze big data and identify data goldmines for their companies. We don't know what we don't know, but the platform knows.

In food services, for example, a company like Whitsons will be able to deliver even more customized data and meals. In fact, customization will be so advanced that a company likely will be able to predict and in turn suggest the exact food with the exact type and amount of nutrients in a single serving that an individual should eat to optimize their personal health. And all delivered via smart phone, smart watch, or smart glasses.[4]

EVOLUTION OF BUSINESS

Such is the power and the evolution of business in a digital and beyond connected world. Experience matters now. But tomorrow's business world takes it to the next level. Experience selling will replace traditional product selling. Intelligence generated by platforms will dissect customer interest and actions, or lack thereof, and generate a best plan of action.

In simple form, think in terms of rideshare companies with their dynamic pricing models. Remember, that's charging higher prices for rides to peak locations and at peak times as adjusted by an algorithm.

Or, another example of experience marketing is Breakwater, the New Jersey–based small and growing cannabis company. To differentiate itself in a crowded market, rather than market its product, the company markets the experience.

Product information management makes more sense than simply selling the product off shelves, virtual and otherwise. It's about giving the consumer information and experience—from how to buy the product to what type of product, and end-to-end product procurement.

All this matters now because with a platform in place, anyone can sell to any user anywhere in the world within regulatory limits because everything is moving to the Cloud. The platform knows the rules and regulations and gives companies the power to sell, ship, deliver service, invoice, collect the money, and even service complaints. And it's all made possible with a digital operating model in place.

With the onset of 5G, 6G, and quantum computing, businesses will be able to become intelligent.

NEXT-GEN OPEN ARTIFICIAL INTELLIGENCE

Another revolution is underway in technology, this time involving language models in artificial intelligence. A language model uses artificial intelligence to predict words in a sequence. For example, when you start typing a message in some programs and apps, those suggested next words are the result of a language model that learns through AI.

Unsupervised

The impossible is possible. Imagine a system that with no human intervention can mine, extract, and learn useful information from all spoken languages and any text ever written. That includes images, audio, and video. That system can then become intelligent enough to analyze the data and use it to speculate, predict, categorize, and further process more data.

With the addition of more technology, all this happens in an instant. Predicting the next words in a sequence is only the beginning. We now can even translate any natural language into code, which eventually will evolve into rapid software development.

Tomorrow people will change their demands even faster. This new generation software will meet those demands just as fast. And there are many more potential ways of utilizing it to automate any task.

Right now we see a race toward building larger language models. All that is required is more training data, computing power, and learning parameters. For example, in the not-so-distant future, a business analyst will be able to model systems, business processes, and workflows, and design interfaces in a live session with the customer, significantly shortening turnaround time.

Someone could also define acceptance test cases and write user stories by feeding examples in the form of preliminary test cases and stories. A quality assurance engineer would be able to write test cases or even automate the automation test scripting.

Possibilities

The future will not only be about speed of execution, but also about a universe of infinite possibilities. This has profound implications in almost every industry. As we experiment more, we will find newer applications.

Some of the most evident uses are human-like intelligent chatbots, websites, or a mobile app maker. For example, insurance needs analysis and underwriting could benefit by deploying intelligent software agents that chat with a user and complete the process with better results than delivered through human intervention.

A fintech company could use the technology to detect and prevent fraud at a level where most of the present technologies fail. Crimes could be prevented before they happen. Art, music, screenplays, videos, and more could be created by almost anyone with access to the advanced technology. Oscar-, Emmy-, or Grammy-grade material could be produced by a wannabe. These are just a few scenarios, and they're only the beginning of the possibilities of this next-generation open AI.

OpenAI, the Company

OpenAI is disruption happening in the software sector. Instead of months and years to write software, it will eventually take a few days or even a few minutes to develop and build.

Typically the software development cycle starts with a customer providing a requirement that then involves several layers of participants who build out the program. The development cycle is like building a house by first laying the foundation, and then brick by brick, wall by wall. OpenAI instead will enable a repository of prefabricated pieces of the software development puzzle. Again, using the house analogy, it's like a prefabricated house with readily available pieces that fit together.

People will consume the software programming codes rather than building line-by-line software codes. What that means when it comes to those business building blocks—experience, process, and data—is that business components become plug-and-play, quality software, bug-free, well-tested, and ready to go. All this shortens the software development cycle even more and enables platform delivery in less time, with less cost, and higher quality outcomes.

THE METAVERSE

Some people refer to *metaverse* as the next-generation internet. More accurately though, the metaverse or meta verse—depending on whose version it is—is an alternative reality or reality digitally transformed. It's what's next online.

Facebook, reborn Meta, is doing it; so are Microsoft and major game producers and upstarts. Think SimCity on steroids, a Fortnite mega-universe, or next-generation Roblox for everyone. For the uninitiated, these are various online games with their own surrounding digital universe that have been available for some time and adored by their younger mobs of fans.

In other words, a metaverse is an online alternative to our real universe—a virtual universe. Instead of physically real people, physically real properties, goods and services, the metaverse is virtual and online. People become avatars.

The bottom line is ultimate choice. Anyone can be who or what they want to be in whatever form; they can speak and act as they like. They can live and interact wherever, however, and whenever they want—and all virtually.

Whatever happens with the metaverse, digitally mature companies will be able to pivot and deliver their goods and services as needed virtually and otherwise.

MAKING SENSE OF IT ALL

What other impossibilities could be possible tomorrow? We could be sitting remotely in a business meeting with holograms next to us. Robots could be the new servers and chefs in the school cafeterias. Neural science may lead to simulated smells as well as better voice technologies—all with the goal of improving the experience.

New Ideas, New Jobs

These innovations are about humans fulfilling their needs by making machines more intelligent to unleash the human potential. Perhaps there will be a robot chef programmed to cook Michelin-star meals.

That doesn't mean the robot will displace the chef. The chef is the creator and simply will create something more and better. After all, someone has to input the data into the machines.

Back to the three elements of the digital operating model—culture, platform, and innovation—no matter where any company is on its digital journey, all three must be present for a successful transformation. And even though we've moved beyond digital, all three still must be present for the growing changes to happen.

New Realities

The future is a world mixed between digital and reality, says Christopher Yin, IT creative thought leader. Mixed reality technologies—including augmented reality applications—are still in their infancy. But they're happening and fast. The maturation process is similar to how the iPhone and iPod changed how the world interacted with music, information, and entertainment. It's not an overnight process and it takes time. The journey already is underway for most of us.

Forget being tethered to a desk. Eventually work will be possible from literally anywhere with just a screen. Imagine tapping your headset or using your voice to augment or completely change your perceived reality. From visual overlays for navigation delivered on your glasses or heads-up display in a vehicle to information presented as you look at things with computer vision, an immersive 360-degree desktop is possible.

With technologies like augmented reality, visual reality, and mixed reality, the user's experience is no longer bound by the traditional user interface known as WIMP: windows, icons, menus, and pointer. Think about how a company could enhance its customers' and customer's customers' experience with real-time mixed reality.

Vehicle makers already count on heads-up displays courtesy of augmented reality. The coffee machine maker has done the same with virtual reality. Customers now can see a 360-degree view of the machine in the setting of their choice.

Anything Is Possible

With such rapid advances in technology, philosophically, all things are possible in the future, agrees IT and product expert Ian Worden. "It's just a matter of time and money. With that guiding principle in place, we can avoid being overly enamored with technology and instead focus on the value equation of deploying technology."

Organizations, he says, should continue to identify competitive differences that create value for their customers knowing that technology can be leveraged to accelerate and enhance those objectives. "It is less important to know which technologies and more important to know how value is created. With clarity on competitive advantage and value creation, technology experts then can help identify the most suitable existing, new, and emerging technologies to achieve the objectives."

Crum & Forster CEO Marc Adee adds his perspective: "I feel like our model lets us look at new technologies when they start to have practical value. RPA hit that threshold several years ago. AI is definitely there now. Blockchain is probably a few years out for us—and then there will be something else. We will be ready for it."

THE JOURNEY

The journey to today's digital operating model (Figure 12.1) has evolved over time. No matter what point along the pathway, though, digital always is about better experiences, more efficient processes, and more reliable data. The iterations of digital's evolution include:

- The 1960s and 1970s was an era of one big computer—the IBM mainframe—processing automation for a business using DB2 as their database.
- The next generation divided big computers into many small computers called minicomputers and the operating model was distributed computing—Unix. Data was stored in tabular format for easy access and shaped into a relational database.
- The internet and web technologies took us on the SMAC (an acronym for social, mobile, analytics, and cloud) or Web 2.0.
- As companies continued to accelerate with distributed computing, it became expensive. The evolution of the sharing economy gave birth to

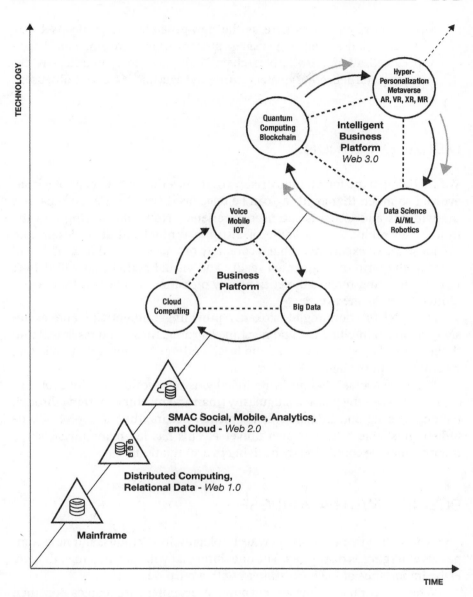

FIGURE 12.1   Digital evolution.

Cloud technologies. The amount of data grew with the combination of structured and unstructured information and became known as Big Data.

- The Cloud platform began to offer the on-demand model of computing and processing power at reasonable costs.

- The future already is here as the new-generation internet—Web 3.0, which includes intelligent business platforms, virtual reality, meta, hyper-personalization, AI/ML, blockchain, and quantum computing—is disrupting and delivering greater security and data under the control of users.

DIGITAL EVOLUTION

We are living in the fourth industrial revolution, a time when technology has evolved so much that anything can be developed, says Yin. What separates the winners and losers is the user experience. Now and moving into the future user retention is a battle of attrition through intuitive design and unique creative experiences that a company provides the end user. This will come in the form of augmented reality and virtual reality that will deliver visualization and replace the current way of using the internet. More commonly that's the metaverse.

With NFTs (nonfungible tokens) providing authenticity and exclusivity, artificial intelligence, and machine learning, those who resist will find themselves playing catchup like the brick-and-mortar stores that balked at e-commerce in the late 1990s, says Yin.

"The metaverse, though in its infancy, is our world digitally evolved," says Yin. "When the point of singularity [man and machine merging through bio-engineering and human enhancements] occurs, the metaverse will be indistinguishable from our own universe. This has led many physicists to theorize that we could already be living in a simulation."

BUSINESS WITH A PURPOSE

The world ahead will witness new technologies, innovations, and new companies emerging as disruptors. The one thing that will stay the same, though, is the importance of business strategy with a purpose.

When a company chases purpose, everything else comes together. Employees—no matter their generation—will choose to work for a company. That company will achieve Level 5 of DOM—continuous digital maturity—and the exponential growth that follows.

As humans we all strive to achieve our potential. Some people are driven, others not so much, but we all like to do well and excel at whatever we do.

In these pages we have seen how purposeful excellence is plausible and possible with the power of the digital operating model in motion. We have seen how culture, business platform, and innovation can work together to drive purpose and make the difference for ourselves, our companies, and others. Combined with unwavering commitment to purpose and deliverable actions, the result is the delivery of intelligent, better, faster, and easier experiences for all of us.

The business platform opens the future to new possibilities, some that haven't yet been imagined. Combine that with what we do know along with imagination, and the power of empathetic, authentic, and the vulnerable digital leaders of tomorrow, and there are no limits to what we can accomplish.

At the end of the day, no matter the business, its size, or industry, if its purpose/commitment is to make the world a better place to live and work, success and profits will follow. Many of today's, and definitely tomorrow's, consumers and customers demand it. The moment you connect purpose with profits, people and companies will want to work with you, period.

PATHWAYS TO GROWTH: A ROUNDUP

- The future is about unleashing the potential of people and businesses to make our lives better.
- A DOM leads to intelligence that delivers consumer happiness with the experience of the platform and is a pathway to becoming a business with purpose. The latter is table stakes for the future and the ticket to exponential growth.
- Changing demographics, markets, and even climate change contribute to next-generation workers' and consumers' passions about sustainability and making the world a better place to live and work.
- As staffing becomes increasingly more difficult in a world changed by COVID-19, some companies continue to look at alternatives like robotics and other automation tools to accomplish certain tasks. The goal can be less dependance on scarce human capital.
- We can think of the future of business in terms of DIEP—an acronym for digital, intelligence (AI and data science combined), experience, and purpose.
- Tomorrow's business world takes experience to the next level. Experience selling will replace product selling. Intelligent business platforms

and hyper-personalization will be the norm. Intelligence generated by platforms will dissect customer interest and actions or lack thereof and generate a best plan of action.

- Open artificial intelligence is another next step. Imagine a system that unsupervised—with no human intervention—can mine, extract, and learn useful information from all spoken languages and any text ever written. That includes images, audio, and video. That system can then become intelligent enough to analyze the data and use it to speculate, predict, categorize, and further process more data.

- Then there's the metaverse, an alternative reality or reality digitally transformed. It's what's next online. Actually, it's already here and has an active e-commerce scene.

- The possibilities are endless. The impossible is possible.

Epilogue

Why *DOM: The Future of Business* Is Your Game Changer

I have spent three decades developing my expertise as a consulting professional—an IT doctor who specializes in business transformation via digital pathways.

I've dealt with all sizes of business and across various industries from the United States and Latin America to the United Kingdom, Europe, India, Middle East, and Australia. And, I know that what works in one company does not work in others as well as what works for one country does not work for others. I've recruited more than 10,000 people in multiple countries and understand the work culture of different parts of the world. I'm not just a consultant either. I and my company have been part of putting together business platforms that help companies generate exponential growth stories.

From that experience, I've identified the common denominators for success. They include the importance of thorough assessments and road maps—As Is and To Be—as discussed throughout this book. Having met thousands of CEOs, the most successful have a growth mindset and are willing to learn and change, too. Hence, the future is about agility and adoption.

Over the years I've also seen more companies fail at achieving digital maturity than succeed. Also as discussed in these pages, it's not about the technology, but rather the people involved. Those who strive for fewer mistakes—who learn from others' past mistakes—are the most successful.

After immersing myself in so many complex situations as an IT doctor, I find simplicity in solving the problems. One size does not fit all, but one approach does solve most problems. When someone is sick, a medical professional assesses the situation, then prescribes a solution.

The future of work is more preventive than prescriptive. In the past, management consultants offered prescriptive solutions—bandage solutions. In our digital age, solutions are more preventative in nature.

Thoughts on the Future of Business

- **To solve problems:** We must approach them as a doctor does an ailing patient—assess the problem, then come up with solutions.

- **In the education sector:** After working with more than 100 universities worldwide, I've learned that all want to teach a relevant curriculum with good professors and deliver exceptional student experience. Why then does each have its own unique and complex IT system? Perhaps there should be one system in the future called "One University System." Everyone can customize it instead of building their platforms.

- **In the food industry:** Food suppliers and manufacturers in schools, universities, hospitals, assisted-living facilities, corporations, events, and restaurants all require ingredients, recipes, menus, and staff. All the food products' nutrition and ingredients are standard. An egg is high in protein; therefore, it's usually used to provide protein in a meal. Why isn't there one global system with all products and their nutrient information that is shared as an ecosystem in the same way airlines maintain flight prices in a centralized system of Sabre and Amadeus?

- **In the fintech payments space:** Digital payments are inevitable, so why don't all countries use a common business platform instead of building separate systems for each government and each industry? It requires extensive customization, but one can reuse the 50% from the out-of-the-box platform.

- **In the insurance sector:** Data play a vital role in the future of the insurance industry. Why isn't there one platform for data science needs that all companies can tap into, again like the airline industry with Sabre and Amadeus?

- **On the manufacturing sector:** Why does everyone create their own products inventory system when it's possible to have a common system?

- **On the preventative versus prescriptive approach to business wellness:** So many consumers today opt to embrace wellness, diet, and exercise to stay healthy instead of getting sick and popping pills as the solution. Similarly in business, the journey to digital maturity begins with the digital operating model as your guide and is the preventative pathway to avoid disruption and to remain relevant and purposeful today and into the future.

- **On the digital platform:** The business platform enables companies to deliver their unique customer experiences and fulfills the purposeful promise of making life easier and better for everyone.

LAST WORDS FOR NOW

Life should be like a flowing river, not a stagnant pond. Along the river we bump into big stones and learn to avoid them while the small stones we pick up and enjoy along the way. The river continuously flows, branches into canals, and merges into the oceans. On the journey it serves many purposes—from creating fertile lands to providing sustenance, transportation routes, and making life better for those around it.

Successful businesses are like the river, and digital transformation the pathway for a company to become relevant now and into the future. When a business connects purpose with profits, everyone benefits.

Endnotes

PREFACE

1. CNN Money. Fortune 500 annual ranking. https://money.cnn.com/maga-zines/fortune/fortune500/2010/full_list/ (accessed 15 January 2022).

   PWC. (2015). Global Top 100 Companies by market capitalisation. (31 March) p. 58. https://www.pwc.com/gx/en/audit-services/capital-market/publica-tions/assets/document/pwc-global-top-100-march-update.pdf (accessed 15 January 2022).

CHAPTER 1

1. Louise Marie M. Cornillez, L.M.M. (1999), "Spice Trade in India." Postcolonial Studies @ Emory. https://scholarblogs.emory.edu/postcolonialstudies/2014/06/21/spice-trade-in-india/ (accessed 12 October 2021).

2. UNESCO. "What Are the Spice Routes." Silk Roads Programme. https://en.unesco.org/silkroad/content/what-are-spice-routes (accessed 12 October 2021).

3. Reuters staff. (2014). China to establish $40 billion silk road infrastructure fund. Reuters (8 November). https://www.reuters.com/article/us-china-diplomacy/china-to-establish-40-billion-silk-road-infrastructure-fund-idUSKBN0IS0BQ 20141108 (accessed 12 November 2021).

4. Peck, R. (2017). Mark Cuban: "Data Is the New Gold." Credit Suisse (22 June). https://www.credit-suisse.com/about-us-news/en/articles/news-and-expertise/mark-cuban-data-is-the-new-gold-201706.html (accessed 12 October 2021).

5. Fryer, V. BigCommerce.com, The history of commerce: from the silk road to modern ecommerce. BigCommerce.com. https://www.bigcommerce.com/blog/commerce/ (accessed 12 November 2021).

CHAPTER 2

1. *Wall Street Journal.* (2013). Nelson Mandela, in his own words. (5 December). https://www.wsj.com/articles/SB10001424127887323949904578537294290182734 (accessed 23 March 2022).
2. IDC. (2020). Digital transformation investments to top $6.8 trillion globally as businesses & governments prepare for the next normal. (8 December). https://www.idc.com/getdoc.jsp?containerId=prMETA47037520 (accessed 4 September 2021).
3. United Nations Population Fund. (2013). World Population to Increase by One Billion by 2025. (12 June). https://www.unfpa.org/news/world-population-increase-one-billion-2025 (accessed 10 January 2022).
4. Mastercard. Mastercard's Purpose Manifesto: Connecting Everyone to Priceless Possibilities. https://www.mastercard.us/content/dam/public/mastercard-com/na/us/en/documents/purpose-manifesto.pdf (accessed 1 December 2021).
5. Mastercard. Featured Topic: Decency. https://www.mastercard.com/news/perspectives/featured-topics/decency/ (accessed 10 October 2021).
6. Leswing, K. (2022). Apple implies it generated record revenue from the app store during 2021. *CNBC* (10 January). https://www.cnbc.com/2022/01/10/apple-implies-it-generated-record-revenue-from-app-store-during-2021-.html (accessed 27 January 2022).

CHAPTER 3

1. Asha Goswami, A. (2017). Life lessons from the Bhagavad-Gita. *The Pioneer* (24 September). https://www.dailypioneer.com/2017/sunday-edition/life-lessons-from-bhagavad-gita.html (accessed 10 January 20222).
2. Ethereal theme. (date unknown). Lessons. *Chanakya.* http://chanakyasstory.blogspot.com/p/lessons.html (accessed 12 September 2021).
3. De Montfort University Higher Education Corporation. (2010). Annual Accounts: 2009–2010. De Montfort University Leicester (December), p. 12. https://www.dmu.ac.uk/documents/about-dmu-documents/university-governance/annual-reports/dmu-annual-accounts-2009-2010.pdf (accessed 2 January 2022).
4. Truong, K. (2019). Microsoft HealthVault is officially shutting down in November. *MedCity News* (8 April). https://medcitynews.com/2019/04/microsoft-healthvault-is-officially-shutting-down-in-november (accessed 12 October 2021).

5. *The Guardian.* (2021). The Best UK Universities 2022—Rankings (11 September). https://www.theguardian.com/education/ng-interactive/2021/sep/11/the-best-uk-universities-2022-rankings (accessed 4 November 2021).

6. Clark, D. (2022). Number of universities and higher education institutions in the United Kingdom from 2010/11 to 2018/19. *Statista* (23 February). https://www.statista.com/statistics/915603/universities-in-the-united-kingdom-uk/ (accessed 4 November 2021).

7. Ntovas, N. (2021). Pod structure: Creating the right team or the perfect outsourcing coverup? (3 March). https://www.linkedin.com/pulse/pod-structure-creating-right-team-perfect-outsourcing-nicholas/ (accessed 28 January 2022).

8. Hendry, E.R. (2013). 7 epic fails brought to you by the genius mind of Thomas Edison. *Smithsonian* (20 November). https://www.smithsonianmag.com/innovation/7-epic-fails-brought-to-you-by-the-genius-mind-of-thomas-edison-180947786/ (accessed 10 January 2022).

9. Ong, J. (2010). Apple co-founder offered his computer design to H-P 5 times. *Apple Insider* (7 December). https://appleinsider.com/articles/10/12/07/apple_co_founder_offered_first_computer_design_to_hp_5_times (accessed 10 January 2022).

10. Mastercard (2021). Mastercard launches new Start Path cryptocurrency and blockchain program for startups. Press release (27 July). https://www.mastercard.com/news/press/2021/july/mastercard-launches-new-start-path-crypto-currency-and-blockchain-program-for-startups (accessed 30 January 2022).

11. Mastercard (2021). Mastercard launches Strive: A global small business initiative to accelerate economic recovery. Press release (22 September). https://www.mastercardcenter.org/press-releases/mastercard-strive (accessed 30 January 2022).

CHAPTER 4

1. Food and Nutrition Service. (2013). Healthy Hunger-Free Kids Act. U.S. Department of Agriculture (20 November). https://www.fns.usda.gov/cn/healthy-hunger-free-kids-act (accessed 6 November 2021).

2. Whitsons Culinary Group. (2021). Whitsons Culinary Group ranks #16 in Food Management's 2021 Top 50; #6 in K-12. https://www.whitsons.com/communication/news/whitsons-culinary-group-ranks-16-food-managements-2021-top-50-6-k-12 (accessed 7 October 2021).

3. Buzalka, M. (2021). The top eight largest K-12 school food service operators: 6.6 Whitsons Culinary Group. *Food Management* (21 April). https://www .food-management.com/print/49519 (accessed 1 August 2021).

CHAPTER 8

1. Kenji Explains, "What Happened to Nokia Phones," Medium.com/StartItUp, April 10, 2020. https://medium.com/swlh/what-happened-to-nokia-2a920b622d52 (accessed 10 May 2021).
2. Sentner-White, S. and Feterik, K. (2020). It's time for healthcare providers to stop faxing. *Cerner* (27 July). https://www.cerner.com/perspectives/its-time-for-health-care-providers-to-stop-faxing (accessed 10 October 2021).

CHAPTER 9

1. Pries, A. (2021). Toys 'R' Us is opening its only U.S. store in N.J. The grand opening is Tuesday. NJ.com (21 December). https://www.nj.com/news/2021/ 12/toys-r-us-is-opening-its-only-us-store-in-nj-the-grand-opening-is-tuesday. html (accessed 2 January 2022).
2. Isaac, M. (2016). Twitter's 4-year odyssey with the 6-second video app Vine. *The New York Times* (28 October). https://www.nytimes.com/2016/10/29/ technology/twitters-4-year-odyssey-with-the-6-second-video-app-vine.html (1 January 2022).
3. La Monica, P.R. (2019). Barnes & Noble is going private after bruising battle with Amazon. CNN (7 June). https://www.cnn.com/2019/06/07/investing/ barnes-and-noble-going-private/index.html (accessed 27 December 2021).
4. Ziegler, C. (2012). Pre- to postmortem: The inside story of the death of Palm and webOS. *The Verge* (5 June 5). https://www.theverge.com/2012/ 6/5/3062611/palm-webos-hp-inside-story-pre-postmortem (accessed 12 September 2021).
5. Ewen, L. (2015). How Sports Authority went bankrupt—and who could be the next to fall. *Fortune* (16 March). https://www.retaildive.com/news/how-sports-authority-went-bankruptand-who-could-be-next-to-fall/415343/ https://fortune .com/2016/06/30/dicks-sports-authority/ (accessed 22 December 2022).
6. London Higher. (2019). London Higher Fact Sheet 2019: Students in Higher Education, 2017/18. https://www.londonhigher.ac.uk/wp-content/uploads/ 2019/07/LdnHigher_HESAStudents2019.pdf (accessed 2 January 2022).

7. Online Master of Athletic Administration. (2020). Virtual training for football is becoming a reality. Ohio University (27 January). https://onlinemasters.ohio.edu/blog/virtual-training-for-football-is-becoming-a-reality/ (accessed 20 October 2021); Designing Digitally (2020). How the NFL uses virtual reality for training (30 January). https://www.designingdigitally.com/blog/how-nfl-uses-virtual-reality-training (accessed 20 October 2021).

8. Sol Rogers, S. (2020). Is immersive technology the future of journalism? *Forbes* (6 February). https://www.forbes.com/sites/solrogers/2020/02/06/is-immersive-technology-the-future-of-journalism/?sh=6272ac317e30 (accessed 12 January 2022).

9. Incao, J. (2018). How VR is transforming the way we train associates. *Walmart Today* (20 September). https://corporate.walmart.com/newsroom/innovation/20180920/how-vr-is-transforming-the-way-we-train-associates (accessed 15 January 2022).

10. Brown, S. (2022). Machine learning, explained. MIT Sloan Management: Ideas Made to Matter (26 January). https://mitsloan.mit.edu/ideas-made-to-matter/machine-learning-explained (accessed 29 January 2022).

11. Stewart, M. (2019). The limitations of machine learning. *Towards Data Science* (29 July). https://towardsdatascience.com/the-limitations-of-machine-learning-a00e0c3040c6 (accessed 22 January 2022).

CHAPTER 10

1. Mastercard. (2016). Mastercard announces acquisition of Vocalink. Press release (21 July). https://newsroom.mastercard.com/press-releases/mastercard-announces-acquisition-of-vocalink/

2. Telford-Reed, N. (2020). The changes real-time payment solutions can bring about. Endava #Payment Talks (7 July). https://www.youtube.com/watch?v=rAlh_lqn6NQ (accessed 18 December 2021).

CHAPTER 11

1. Jovanovic, B. (2022). Internet of things statistics for 2022: Taking things apart. DataProt (8 March). https://dataprot.net/statistics/iot-statistics/.

2. Bonnell, S. 4 leaders who won by following their instincts (despite being told they were crazy). *Inc.* https://www.inc.com/sunny-bonnell/how-to-follow-your-instincts-in-business-even-when-people-say-youre-crazy.html (accessed 5 January 2022).

3. Chew, S.L. (2018). Myth: We only use 10% of our brains. Association for Psychological Science (29 August). https://www.psychologicalscience.org/teaching/myth-we-only-use-10-of-our-brains.html (accessed 8 September 2021); Boyd, R. (2008). Do people only use 10 percent of their brains? *Scientific American* (7 February). https://www.scientificamerican.com/article/do-people-only-use-10-percent-of-their-brains/ (accessed 8 September 2021).

4. Petrov, C. (2022). 50+ voice search stats to help you rethink your strategy in 2021. Tech Jury (4 January). https://techjury.net/blog/voice-search-stats/#gref (accessed 5 January 2022).

5. Petrov, C. (2022). 49 stunning internet of things statistics 2021 (the rise of IoT). Tech Jury (4 January). https://techjury.net/blog/internet-of-things-statistics/ (accessed 5 January 2022).

6. Jovanović, B. (2021). Internet of things statistics for 2021. DataProt (24 March). https://dataprot.net/statistics/iot-statistics/ (accessed 17 May 2021).

7. Biospace. (2021). IOT in healthcare market to reach USD 260.75 billion by 2027: Reports and data (8 July). https://www.biospace.com/article/iot-in-healthcare-market-to-reach-usd-260-75-billion-by-2027-reports-and-data/ (accessed November 2021).

8. IHL Group. Research and Advisory: Product Overview. https://www.ihlservices.com/product/inventorydistortion/ (accessed 7 November 2021).

CHAPTER 12

1. Centers for Disease Control and Prevention. Mental health and stress-related disorders. https://www.cdc.gov/climateandhealth/effects/mental_health_disorders.htm (accessed 4 November 2021).

2. McCrindle. Gen Z and Gen Alpha Infographic Update. https://mccrindle.com.au/insights/blogarchive/gen-z-and-gen-alpha-infographic-update/ (accessed 3 December 2021).

3. LatentView Analytics. (2021). How data science, AI, and machine learning work together (20 July). https://www.latentview.com/blog/how-data-science-ai-and-machine-learning-work-together/ (accessed 20 January 2022).

4. The Economist (2021). What if everyone's nutrition was personalised? (30 July). https://www.economist.com/what-if/2021/07/03/what-if-everyones-nutrition-was-personalised (accessed 3 January 2022).

Appendix/Rajesh Sinha: A Digital Entrepreneur's Journey

Purpose first and happiness will follow. . .

I remember walking along holding my dad's hand at age seven and asking him how to become a "king." To me as a child, a "king" meant protector, caretaker, and caregiver. I would read comic books about the kings who disguised themselves and roamed the cities and countrysides to find the real problems of their people.

I asked my dad, how did someone become a leader with the power to control their own destiny? He told me that the "kings" of modern times are those people who run countries, politicians, and business leaders. He gave the examples of Tata and Birla, leading business families who owned many companies in India at that time.

I was born in a small town in Muzaffarpur, Bihar, in northeastern India, far away from the frenetic financial hub of Mumbai or the eclectic aura of New Delhi. My dad was a civil engineer in a lifetime job with the government. He worked in a system fraught with corruption yet demonstrated extreme honesty that I still admire today.

He also had entrepreneurial aspirations and started many part-time businesses throughout his life. One of those businesses was a private boarding school. I was about 11 and remember accompanying him on the search for the right building to house the school. I even helped him hang the sign on the gate in front of the school—Delhi National Public School, R.C. Sinha, Chairman. I felt such a sense of pride, inspiration, and purpose when we raised the sign, especially since my initials, like my dad's, are R.C.S.

As long as the sign hung, every time I walked under it, I felt pride of accomplishment and importance, feelings that are so much a part of being an entrepreneur. Back then, owning a business may have been the pipe-dream of a child, but the lessons I learned about business were very real and still remain with me today.

Many people from our city did not have the opportunity or could not afford a good education. I remember my dad wouldn't take money from the genuinely poor who wanted to learn but could not pay. The importance of purpose before profits mattered to me and my family early on.

Later, my dad's school ran into many operational as well as management and leadership issues. My dad allowed emotions and gossip from others to interfere with business decisions, clouding the school's pathway to success. I used to sit in the school's kitchen and listen to the cooks complain about wage disparities and gossip about the teachers' inability to teach.

In retrospect, the biggest learning from that experience was people on the front lines understand best the on-the-ground realities and challenges in a business. Leaders must listen. My father—with his top-down leadership style—did not. A good "king," after all, collects feedback from his constituents.

That doesn't mean, though, I haven't made some of the same mistakes. The two biggest differences, however, are that I know the importance of staying connected with employees and I understand that failures are learnings.

When I built my own business—Fulcrum Digital—I made several mis-takes. But one thing I consistently got right was staying connected with employees. Even now, with nearly 1,200 employees worldwide, I work hard to know and listen to the people in the company—from those at the front desks of our worldwide offices to the CEO. So many of our employees have been a part of our teams for years in part because of that connection and, I hope, my willingness to listen.

College and Career Choice

My dad wanted me to follow him and become a civil engineer, but even as a teen, I had big dreams—a growth mindset. I wanted to do something new and different and with purpose, so I chose instead to study what at the time was the new emerging field of computer science. I also knew that it would provide me an opportunity to travel the world in search of opportunities because it was going to be the next big thing.

The year was 1989 when I left for Amravati University in Maharashtra, near Mumbai on the west coast of India. For vacations I returned to work at my dad's latest entrepreneurial venture, a furniture dealership. That's where I learned customer management skills that were the foundation for how we treat our customers worldwide today.

Choice and Direction

As with digital transformation, choices we make affect our outcomes. When I graduated from college in 1993, I chose to begin my computer science career in Mumbai, the country's financial center. I sold my engineering compass set to give me a small amount of cash, and set out for Mumbai. I didn't have enough money for the train ticket, so like many others, I dodged the ticket collector and made it to the city.

Rather than live outside the city, I chose the center of it all—Andheri—where I felt I could grow faster, and I did. There were many days I could only afford the few cents for one meal—vada pav (deep-fried potato dumpling sandwich) or idli (made from ground rice and dal). We all must begin our journey somewhere.

My first job was in management consulting sales for a software solutions provider. I earned $50 a month. But, as always, my choices weren't about making money. Rather it was the experience and the product that mattered.

This also is where I first learned the importance of As Is and To Be in terms of the DOM journey. Satish Kini, my first boss and a veteran of IBM, shared that wisdom as well as taught me the fundamentals of management consulting. When I left about a year later, my salary had increased to $600 a month and I was on my way.

I then moved to selling Computer Associates' product, Unicenter, and Informix's relational database software, both distributed by L&T and Silverline. I changed jobs, again not for the money, but to chase bigger dreams and the hottest software of the moment, upgrading my knowledge, skills, and expertise in the process.

New York, New Life, New Business

In 1997, I moved to the United States and began selling software services in New Jersey.

I landed at John F. Kennedy International Airport from Mumbai on 7 December 1997. I came alone—my wife, Vandhana, remained in Mumbai until I was able to set up a rental apartment. The day after I landed, I remember attending an IT conference at Jacob Javits Center in New York City and winning many prizes at various vendor booths. It must have been a positive sign.

In those first years as a salesperson, I made lots of phone calls, and because we lived in a small apartment and no one had cell phones at the time, I used to make those calls on public telephones. Those cramped, hot telephone booths were my "office." I would find public phones located on small backstreets to avoid the traffic noise and make as many calls as possible pitching my products in search of sales.

In 1999, when Accurum, the company I was with at the time, was sold to Kanbay (now Cap Gemini), I decided to start my own company.

I saw a need and an opportunity. I also saw the software side of the business from India, and now in the United States, and had a clearer picture of the entire ecosystem. That picture revealed a gap in services provided by large Indian and U.S. companies. Indian companies provided low-cost software programming services while U.S. companies charged high dollars. Both seemed to ignore the midsize market that wanted value at the right price.

Also at the time, most companies and providers were deeply involved in the scramble to become Y2K compliant. Instead of joining the pack in pursuit of that short-term goal, I chose to take the value creation (long-term) route with my company. It was a big risk, but I also knew it was a turning point in my life. I wanted to transform lives and be part of designing the future of the industry—a tall order for a young Indian immigrant. Vandhana had a good job, so I figured that if my business failed, at least she would be earning money and could take care of the family.

At the time, I hadn't realized the importance of learning from other CEOs first before starting a business.

Tough Lessons

Everything hasn't been smooth sailing. In those early years, I was bullish, cocky, and overconfident. I was enamored with my success so young—although it wasn't conceit, but rather pride.

I thought I knew everything, but quickly found out otherwise. I made lots of mistakes. But making mistakes is about recognizing them quickly, having the wisdom and fluidity to fix those mistakes, and learning from them. After all, as I've discussed in these pages, failure is an important part of the journey to success.

Like father, like son, too. I allowed emotion to cloud my judgment. Instead of a thorough assessment of the options and opportunities and a road map— sound planning—to dictate my actions, I listened to others and allowed my company to get caught up in too much expansion in products and offices too fast. We opened offices in London; San Francisco; São Paulo, Brazil; Buenos Aires, Argentina; and Mumbai and Pune in India.

When we raised the signboard on top of the building in Pune, I had that same sense of accomplishment as when as a child we raised the signboard on my father's school building. But the incredible feeling did not last long. While we had done what I thought at the time was thorough planning, we miscalculated the cost of running and operating the building in Pune. The small building was in a software jungle surrounded by behemoths with many times our earnings. With the building came big operational challenges that, at the time, were tough.

As a teen, I had criticized many of the emotional decisions made by my father. Yet here I was, my company facing its biggest challenges—a lack of foresightedness, overconfidence, and more. But one powerful trait I did have that I had learned long ago as a child listening to the employees complain at my father's school was staying connected with the people. That saved our company. When people know you care, they will care for you when you need them.

I'm reminded of something the headmaster of The Lawrenceville (New Jersey) School said to my son's high school graduating class—be nice to all while climbing the ladder of success because you will meet the same people on your way down.

Instead of a few helping hands, we had hundreds helping us to land on our feet, and we did. All the founding and long-term employees played a pivotal role in our survival and helped us grow the company to where it is today.

Our firm has been growing exponentially for the last five years. I owe this success to past and present employees and customers who helped us learn their business and become long-term partners. We are a family, too.

Words of Wisdom

Now, I look to other CEOs, fellow leaders, and others to learn from them. Looking back, I wish I had done this earlier. But it's never too late to grow and change and listen and learn.

On the importance of trust. We built a great culture at Fulcrum Digital that revolves around trust. Customers and employees trust our vision, passion, and value creation; thus, they become long-term partners.

On authenticity and vulnerability. While running the business, I realized that people are smarter than we think. It is better to ask for help instead of projecting we know it all. I give full credit for this learning to my wife, son, and company CEO—a great friend all these years.

Successful leaders in today's and tomorrow's digital world are those who embrace vulnerability and authenticity, and who care.

On continually learning. Life is all about subjective and transformative learning. As a part of YPO (Young President Organization, a network of 30,000 CEOs and entrepreneurs), I learn a lot from my colleagues. The Harvard President's Program taught me how to operate and grow a business. I continue to attend the program and learn from the best minds in the world.

On the journey. The lotus is one of the most beautiful flowers, with petals that open one by one. Yet the lotus only grows in mud. To grow and gain wisdom, first you must deal with the mud—the obstacles and challenges.

About the Website

For more information, advice, and guidance—including free, downloadable templates and workbooks—check out www.DigitalOperatingModel.org. Hopefully, the information can be your first steps to help you and your company on the DOM journey to digital maturity.

Index

Page numbers followed by *f* refer to figures.